## Endorsements

"Do you want a job? A good job? You need to turbocharge your job search with the inside secrets that Eleanor has gained through over 20 years of successful experience showing people just like you how to land the right job FAST. This labor market is different. You need a different strategy. This book will give you a game plan to follow to win!"

—Robert Allen, bestselling author
*Nothing Down, Nothing Down for Women,*
*Creating Wealth, Multiple Streams of Income,*
*One Minute Millionaire, Cracking the Millionaire Code,*
*Cash in a Flash: Fast Money in No Time*

"The job market has changed. You must update your job search and get the right tools for success in this labor market and in this economy. You will get the competitive edge in your job search when you read *The NEW Rules of Job Search—How to Land an Executive Job in the New Economy* with Eleanor Sweet, nationally recognized Executive Job Search Expert."

—Kurt Mortensen, author of
*Maximum Influence and Persuasion IQ*

"Eleanor Anne Sweet applies her tried-and-true methods for executive placement to an important new resource for navigating through today's choppy job market. Sweet's detailed, easy-to-follow guide doesn't just show you how to land a job. It shows you how to resume a career."

—Peter Gian, editor-in-chief,
*HomeWor*

"I've known Eleanor for many years—both as a candidate and a client. I can honestly say she's one of the best recruiters/career coaches there is in the business. She's not only a subject matter expert in job search, but also applies what she teaches to real live career situations. She has a tremendous amount of integrity and is driven to achieve great results for her clients/candidates. You would be crazy not to consider her for your career search needs. She has a deep knowledge of product categories and companies. In addition she is extremely networked in with many people. Please take the time to get to know Eleanor and what she can do for you. I guarantee you won't be sorry."

—Rick S., Atlanta, Georgia

"Eleanor has more connections than the soundboard at a Coldplay concert. And if you're going to be a Career Coach/Headhunter, nothing is more important. The reason she knows so many people—people who will gladly take her call— is that she not only knows her field, she gives everyone her full attention and respect. In a field littered with charlatans, money-grabbing Websites and late arrivers, Eleanor is the real deal."

—Bob Simon, Akron, Ohio

"Eleanor possesses the best combination of qualities for an executive recruiter and mentor for candidates. She is communicative and available, but always honest and up-front with clients and candidates alike. She is an excellent coach and works hard to prepare candidates for the challenges of the job search and ultimate interviewing process. In her coaching program for candidates she provides them with the tools necessary to identify opportunities in the hidden jobs market. I have personally worked with Eleanor as a candidate and client and found her to conduct her practice with the utmost integrity. She is always at the top of her profession and a pleasure to work with."

—Dan S., Cleveland, Ohio

"I am anxiously awaiting the release of Eleanor's new book that is coming out shortly. I have worked with Eleanor numerous times over the past few years. She is a professional that is truly committed to helping individuals with your job search. She supplies great support and information that is critical for a successful job search. Based on my experience working with her there is no doubt that her book will be a success. If you are looking to work with a recruiter I would highly recommend Eleanor's talents."

—Alan M., Orlando, Florida

"Professionalism is foremost when it comes to making reference to Eleanor. Her knowledge of the marketplace and the various ways in order to approach the present day environment allows an employment candidate to realize that her path for success is key and does work. Her seminars and consultive guidance is worth more than gold. Her directives and thought initiating visions have helped me gain a more defined path and direction in which I have landed a Director of Sales and Marketing position. Down to earth terms, everyday life situations and personal experiences are conveyed during her lectures. One can only leave to go out and make it happen. Eleanor is truly the best take advantage of her outstanding abilities."

—Ira S., Centereach, New York

"I highly recommend Eleanor as an excellent recruiter. She has a very enthusiastic and energetic personality and I felt an immediate connection with her. She may work for the client but really cares about the candidate. Eleanor is very thorough and has excellent follow up and follows through. A true professional."

—Marguerite D., Pittsburgh, Pennsylvania

# The NEW Rules of
# JOB SEARCH

## How to Land an Executive Job in the New Economy

### ELEANOR ANNE SWEET

*The Executive Job Search Expert*™

Sweet Success books may be purchased for educational, business, or sales promotional use. For information please write: Special Market Department, Sweet Success Publishing, 200 Applebee Street, Suite 213, Barrington, Il 60010

First Sweet Success paperback edition published 2012 Sweet Success is trademarked and The Job Search Experts is a registered trademark.

First Edition

Library of Congress Control Number: 2012903926

ISBN: 978-0-9852464-0-2

Cover and Interior design: 1106 Design, LLC

Publisher's Cataloging-In-Publication Data

*This book is dedicated to Ramon Jan Elias,*
*my wonderful father, the first author in our family.*
*He was a man who loved his fellow mankind*
*and lived his life with integrity and honor.*
*He was a true renaissance man and one of the*
*most gracious people I have ever known.*
*This one's for you, Dad.*

May 16, 1925–March 12, 2004

# CONTENTS

# ACKNOWLEDGMENTS

I WOULD LIKE TO EXTEND my deepest gratitude and thanks to the people who helped me with my journey in creating this book. First I want to thank my family, Pete, Meredith, and Jonathan, for all their support and patience while I worked many weekends and late nights to make this vision come to life.

It is my belief that all major passages and projects are accomplished only with the inspiration and support of others. I would like to thank several of my mentors who assisted me with this passage of my life.

First I would like to thank Robert Allen and Mark Victor Hansen for writing their book, *Cash in a Flash,* which inspired me to create this book. The book you hold in your hands allows me to finally be able to reach out and extensively serve more people with my job search expertise.

In addition, I would like to thank some of my mentors and professional coaches, Brian Tracy, Alex Mandossian, Tim Paulson, Bob Burg, Kurt Mortensen, Robert Skrob, and Jack Canfield, for their continued support in challenging me to constantly improve myself to better serve all the job seekers who look for my assistance with their job search challenges.

I would like to thank Elijah Litscher, Brett Young John Merkle, Kathy Kehrli, Michele DeFilippo, Ronda Rawlins, and all the people at Lightning Source for their professional expertise with my websites and the production of this book.

I have included a link of the contact information for above-mentioned professionals in the back of the book.

I would also like to acknowledge all the job seekers I am currently working with as well as all those I have helped over the years. The list is too long to individually recognize everyone here, but please know that there is a little piece of all of you in this book. Thank you for sharing your dreams, struggles, and triumphs with me. You continued to validate the solutions I shared with you through your individual successes. You also encouraged me to share this information with everyone and not just a select group of job seekers. I feel blessed to have been able to help you and humbly look forward to continuing to serve you. I am here for you always. I believe in you!

Last I would like to thank my personal support team of Aunt Helena, Ann Lax, Joyce Braun, Caroline Horn, Cyndi Evans, Clay Farnsworth, Rick Steinbrenner, Sharon Stagnito, Jean Williams, Stacy Sekinger, Clare Sideman, Angela McKiernan, and everyone for their wonderful support cheering me on through this project.

From the bottom of my heart, thank you, everyone, for your wonderful help and support. I appreciated every single one of you. You have all made a difference in my life and helped me to become a better person.

# Secret Advice from the Executive Job Search Expert™

THE RULES OF THE GAME have changed. If you don't understand how the job search game has changed, then you are not going to succeed with your job search. You will just be wasting your time, spinning your wheels, and not getting hired.

This book is written for you, the executives who have found yourselves challenged in ways you never dreamed of in this current labor market.

How many times have you posted a resume on line and never heard back from anyone?

How many of you are still waiting for someone to return your calls?

*If you have not been getting the results you would like in landing a new job, then this is the book for you.*

*Insanity is doing the same thing over and over again*
*And expecting different results!*
—ALBERT EINSTEIN

It is time to change your job search process.

1

In this book I share with you my new professional Job Search Success System for how to land a job in this new economy.

If you follow the steps I outline, you *will* succeed in landing a job in this new labor market. *You need to believe in yourself first. Then you must take action and have an unwavering desire and commitment to succeed with your job search!*

All you have to do is decide what job you're realistically best suited for, believe you can land that job, believe you deserve it, and follow the strategy outlined in this book.

An eye-opening statistic is that 55–84% of those currently employed are unhappy in their current positions (Conference Board Study and Right Management Study). The majority of these people will be looking for a new job within the next 12 months—on top of those who are currently looking.

So how do you land the job over everyone else? This is a job search system that, when worked properly, will put you way ahead of the pack of other job seekers.

In this book, I give you the basic/functional tools and the inner game tools, followed by the strategic tools, marketing tools, and outer game tools, and finally salary negotiations strategies.

**The first two chapters in this book are the most important chapters! If you do not have your inner game in order, you are not going anywhere in your job search. Without a positive mindset, an intense belief in yourself, and belief in your goal, you will not succeed in your job search.**

Basically the game plan is to focus on your target companies, then networking, then hidden job market ideas, and recruiters last.

I realize that this may not be what you want to hear. I know that it's easier to spend your time just posting your resume on the internet, sending it to a bunch of recruiters, and then sitting back and waiting for people to contact you.

That simply does not work in the new economy. The sooner you realize that, the sooner you will be ahead of the majority of the other job seekers.

This is a market where you are squarely in the driver's seat, and THE ONLY DRIVER. If you are not willing to take the bull by the horns, you will still keep getting the same results, basically little or no activity.

Who the heck am I? I am lady who has been a professional executive recruiter for over 24 years. I am a no-nonsense lady who is a straight shooter—I tell it like it is. I am "The Executive Job Search Expert™." I know how to get the job done, which in this case is how to help you get a job in this current labor market!

In addition, I was unemployed when I relocated to Chicago as a bride after marriage and then when Salton got sold. My husband has been unemployed twice in the last five years. I understand firsthand how to land a job through 24 years of personal and professional experience.

I wrote this book because my heart was being ripped out by everyone I have been unable to help in this current labor market through my executive search firm. With this economy, there are more people looking for jobs than ever before and fewer jobs than ever.

The bottom line is you have a goal: to get a new job. I feel my job, from both a professional and moral standpoint, is to share with you how to achieve that goal, even if some cases it means doing it without my professional help. The most important thing is for you to reach your goal: to land that next great job for you and your family!

Next, I must confess that I left out one very important trade secret from this book by mistake. If you want to know one of the best-kept trade secrets regarding your job search, go to www.thejobsearchexperts.com/bonus-trade-secret/.

This is the secret the other recruiters will not tell you. I think it is in your best interest to understand how the game is really played by the recruiters. That way, you can work it to your advantage, not hurt yourself. Over the years, I have shared this information with every job seeker I have come in contact with.

I created www.TheJobSearchExperts.com to reach out further in helping you, the job seeker, with job search seminars, products, home study courses, and coaching programs to try to help you achieve your job search goal more quickly.

The new rules of getting a job in this new economy are to manage your own job search first and then contact the recruiters *after* you have made all your own contacts through networking, hidden jobs, and your target company list.

When you have finished all those parts of your job search, then—and only then—contact the recruiters. You must tell the recruiters what companies you have already contacted yourself directly to avoid any professional embarrassment for either you or the recruiter.

I know this book is the answer to how you can land a job in this new economy. I know the process outline herein will require more effort on your part, but that is the nature to this current unique labor market. This is the worst labor market this country has seen in the last 29 years. (I know I am not telling you anything you do not know already.)

This is a book written by a professional recruiter with over 24 years of experience in helping executives land great jobs. Some recruiters will not be happy that I am sharing these trade secrets with you. That's fine by me. I feel your success is what matters the most.

You will find this book rich with great content. Do not become overwhelmed, anxious, or worried that there is too much information and you cannot handle it.

The answer is, "How do you eat an elephant?" "One bite at a time."

Take one chapter at a time. Whenever you find yourself emotionally overwhelmed with the process, go back to reread Chapter 2, "How to Keep a Positive Mindset in Challenging Times."

If you discover you are really, really overwhelmed, then contact me at sweet@TheJobSearchExperts.com or 847-304-4500 regarding additional information on my personal or group coaching programs. They will supply a more structured, disciplined, and supportive process that may work better for you. In addition, they provide more in-depth content that you may prefer.

Thank you for reading this Introduction. (I rarely read introductions of books.) If you have read this far, I know you are truly committed to your job search. You are going to be my next success story! Go to this link for a special bonus: www.thejobsearchexperts.com/extra-reader-gift/. It's my way of thanking you for reading this section.

Please know that I want the best for all of you. I want you to land that next great job that you and your family are excited about.

Understand that with this new economy, you may also need to view your next professional job through different eyes than perhaps you would have before this deep recession.

The market is coming back. Stay with it and do not give up.

I wish you continued good luck and success with your job search and with landing that next great job. I believe in you!

Warmly,

*Eleanor*

Eleanor Anne Sweet,
The Executive Job Search Expert™.

The Expert in Executive Job Search Solutions. ™
P.S. Keep me posted at sweet@thejobsearchexperts.com.

PART 1

# Your Inner Game

# CHAPTER 1

# Job Search Tips 4.0
# At the Starting Gate

*I am not discouraged, because every wrong*
*attempt discarded is another step forward.*
—THOMAS EDISON

TO ACHIEVE ANYTHING IN LIFE, one must start with the basics, and finding a new job is no exception. So let's start this whole new phase of your life off by talking about some of the primary elements of a good strong job search campaign. During the job search process, there is so much that is out of your control. I want to share with you some areas that *you **can** control* right off the bat. I know I'm breaking protocol here by giving you the bad news first, but I feel it's important that we first look at the most common causes of job search failure. Don't let that word scare you, though. We're going to concentrate on the areas where you're in complete control of that failure. Once we've put you in the driver's seat, we'll review the areas in which you will personally be able to have more positive impact on your job search and, in turn, effect a positive outcome!

## Working on the Inner Game—15 Reasons
## People Fail with Their Job Search

It's time to take a close, candid look at you and what you've been accomplishing, or perhaps more importantly not been accomplishing, with your job search . . . for whatever reason.

Let's start by examining the most common causes of failure when conducting a job search campaign. Notice that **you have complete control over changing** all of these areas:

1. **Lack of a clear and well-defined vision of the type of position you're seeking**

   In order to succeed in your job search, you need to have a clear idea in mind of the definite type of job you want to land. Possessing this type of clarity, of course, assumes that you have a realistic understanding of your professional background up to this point. It also assumes that you know what type of employment positions you should realistically be considering and applying for.

   Now is the time to do a professional inventory review of both yourself and your job search. Ask yourself, "What are the three most important traits or characteristics I'm looking for in my next ideal, yet realistic, position or company?"

   Write on an index card or piece of paper what these three traits or characteristics are that you're looking for. If you are able to rank them, that is even better. You will need to refer to this information throughout your job search process to make sure the positions you are interviewing for match your "wish" list. It will also make sense to consider revising this list as your job search progresses.

   As you do so, remind yourself of what you liked the most and least in your last three jobs. This will lead you to avoid areas that did not work out for you in your previous employment situations.

## 2. Lack of ambition to aim above mediocrity

There is no hope for the job seeker who is indifferent and unmotivated in their job search. There is only hope for those who are willing to pay the price of being truly committed to their job search, by refusing to give up trying. You must be truly committed and motivated to succeed with your job search!

## 3. Lack of self-discipline

Discipline comes through self-control. Exhibiting self-control means you must push aside all the negative thoughts that creep up on you during your job search. You must also be disciplined in how you manage your time not only each day but throughout the entire job search process.

Before you can control conditions, you must first be able to control yourself. Self-mastery is the hardest job you'll ever tackle, but the effort is well worth it. If you cannot create the self-discipline to manage yourself and your job search, you will not have a good strong employment quest. The stronger your self-discipline and follow-up the faster you will land that next great job you are looking for!

## 4. Procrastination

Don't put off important job search tasks for tomorrow that you can do today—particularly those related to follow-up and follow-through. Procrastination is the most common cause of failure. Every duty you defer is a missed opportunity.

To simplify your job search initiatives, remember to document your phone calls, meetings, interviews, and follow-up conversations in your Excel spreadsheet. To help you with this process, I am providing as Bonus Material an Excel spreadsheet that I have designed for your job search.

5. **Lack of persistence**

Most job seekers are good starters but poor finishers. When it comes to job search endeavors, they begin well but often fail to stay the course. Truth be told, a lot of job seekers give up at the first signs of defeat.

There is no substitute for persistence. Failure cannot survive where there is persistence. Do not allow failure the victory; do not give up!

Of all the important job search areas, I feel that this one tops the list of those that should not be taken lightly. No matter what, you need to keep persevering. Regardless of what roadblocks you encounter, keep trying; do not give up. Success is just around the corner. You never know which name, lead, contact, or networking phone call will lead you to your next job.

6. **Lack of a well-defined power of decision**

Job seekers who succeed often reach decisions quickly but can adapt on a dime. The job seeker who cannot make a timely decision and then changes their mind frequently will quickly tend to experience weaker job search results.

7. **Being overwhelmed with fear**

When you find yourself overwhelmed with fear, you will feel like you are being forced to fight an uphill battle. To steer clear of this disadvantage, you must manage the fear in your heart. The successful job seeker will look fear straight in the eye and laugh in its face.

Every time you feel fear coming on, just go through a list of the 5 things you are grateful for in your life. As you feel the gratitude and joy over your blessings, the fear will be driven away. (See the chapter on How to Keep a Positive Mindset in Challenging Times.)

While you're at it, thank the higher authority in your life for the abundance you've been given. Remind yourself that you are working to recreate job satisfaction in your life.

8. **Being overly cautious**

   The job seeker who will not take any chances generally has to accept whatever is left behind by others. Life itself is filled with an element of chance. You will need to push outside of your comfort zone to beat the competition and create an advantage for yourself in your job search.

9. **Carrying superstition and prejudice**

   Superstition is a form of fear and ignorance. Job seekers who are successful with their job search process keep an open mind and are not afraid of anything. They do not discount a job lead or suggestion until they have thoroughly researched and verified the credibility of the idea. At that point, they then have an action plan to either pursue the job lead or not, based on valid information.

10. **Lack of focus and concentration of effort**

    Concentrate all your efforts on one definite, chief aim. It is better to finish one of your goals on a daily basis than try to accomplish them all and not complete a single one. Focus on one at a time and follow it through to fruition.

11. **Lack of enthusiasm**

    Organizations like to hire enthusiastic candidates who have effectively expressed a desire to work for them. If you don't express excitement during an interview, you will not be convincing to the hiring authority.

12. **Intolerance**

    You cannot have a closed mind in today's job market. Being closed-minded shows that you are not open to new ideas, learning, or growing. Some people also might perceive this trait in you as a sign of inflexibility. Organizations do not hire inflexible people.

13. **Intentional dishonesty**

There is no substitute for honesty. A force of circumstances over which one has no control could render a job seeker temporarily dishonest, without permanent damage. Don't fall into such a trap.

Always put true information on your resume, job applications, references, and all correspondences. If you lie in any of these areas and your untruthfulness is found out after you are hired, it could be solid grounds for termination.

14. **Coming off as being egotistical or vain**

Self-absorption is a real turnoff and a red flag during the interview process. Be careful of using your pride and ego as armor when you're feeling vulnerable. Always present yourself honestly and genuinely. You must always appear authentic. Employers hire those individuals they like, know, and trust.

15. **Guessing instead of thinking**

"Shooting from the hip" and making guesses during either a phone or face-to-face interview will quickly knock you out of the running. Remember to do your company, competitive, and point-of-sales research in advance of any type of one-on-one meeting. Be thoroughly prepared for every meeting.

**RECAP:** You have the ability to control all 15 of these Major Causes of Job Search Failure. Look at them, take action, take control, and re-evaluate how you stack up in all of these areas. There are bound to be some in which you can improve. Take one specific area and work on it for the next 21 days. If you are consistent, at the end of those 21 days your improvement in that area should become an established habit.

## 15 Tips to a Successful Job Search

1. Get focused on the type of job you're seeking.

2. Create a new resume or update/edit a pre-existing resume to match your current job search campaign.

   I'm firm believer in multiple versions of your resume, with a different one to serve each of the various job opportunities you're considering. Create a customized resume to focus on the skill sets specifically listed in each job listing you're applying for. Also, when it comes to the length of your resume, less is better for your initial submissions. Try to keep it to two pages. You can take the longer version (two to three pages) to the actual interview.

3. Create a list of target companies/industries you would like to work for.

   I suggest you start with 20 companies in your "A" list and then add 100 to 200 more along with all their contact information to your "B" and "C" lists.

   Gather all the appropriate contact information you will need to follow up on during your job search campaign. I advise creating this information in Microsoft Excel if you are familiar with that software. Set up different spreadsheets for various industries. I have designed for you a suggested Excel template to use. You will find this template as reader Bonus Material at the end of this chapter for you to access and use throughout your job search process.

4. Send you resume to the appropriate contact person on your list.

   When in doubt, my suggestion is to send it to the president of the organization. From there, it should get passed down to the appropriate department. By taking such an approach, you'll also have the added benefit of the president being aware of your paperwork internally.

Given the high number of people who are currently looking for a job in today's highly competitive job market, I recommend mailing or faxing your resume. Doing so will give your paperwork more visibility. Arrange it so that your cover letter and resume arrive on Tuesday, Wednesday, or Thursday for the simple fact that people tend to have more time in the middle of the week to devote to reading all their correspondence.

5. Work on your "Visual Brand."

When interviewing, make sure you have a professional business suit that fits you. Now is the time to make sure you have your corporate attire in order. I suggest you try everything on in advance to make sure it fits properly and still works for you.

This may sound like an obvious thing, but since the current corporate climate tends to be "business casual," most people's professional business attire has been sitting in the back of their closet for quite some time. As a result, it may not currently fit the way it did when they originally purchased it.

If you have gained some weight you've been meaning to get rid of, now would be a good time to lose a couple of pounds and start working out. (Check with your doctor prior to undertaking any new intense exercise program.)

6. Make sure your business portfolio is complete and up to date.

I always suggest taking your professional portfolio to the first interview in case it is requested. However, it is more traditional to present your portfolio on the second or third interview. Then it's expected that it will be shared and time is allotted for the presentation of it during the interviewing process.

7. Apply for jobs on the internet that interest you and that are fairly realistic in their qualifications relative to your professional background.

    Save copies of which jobs you have submitted a resume to online. Document which organizations you have applied to as well as appropriate contact information for follow-up on your Excel spreadsheet.

    My suggestion is to respond to job postings about two to three days after the initial posting. At this point, H.R. and the recruiters will still be interviewing for the position and your resume will get noticed more. Understand that most postings, particularly in this tight labor market, will easily receive about 350 resume responses.

8. Create a list for executive recruiters who specialize in your area of expertise.

    Create an Excel spreadsheet that contains recruiters' contact information. See "myResumeAgent" on the www.TheJobSearchExperts.com website (www.thejob searchexperts.com/my-resume-agent/). This tool, which comes from Kennedy Publishers of the Directory of Executive Recruiters, will assist you in emailing your resume to recruiters. This tool has six job function areas and six industries to pick from.

9. Send your resume to recruiters as an email attachment.

    That way they are able to scan the resume into their database.

10. Approximately seven days after your initial submission, start following up by phone with both the recruiters and the company contacts regarding the resumes you mailed.

11. Continue following up about every 30 days to check on the status of the job posting or with recruiters who may have new clients.

12. When you get your first interview, be it via phone or face-to-face, make sure you do your homework about the position, hiring authority, company, competitors, and ranking in the marketplace.

    From a professional standpoint, I consider the primary goal of a phone interview to be getting asked in for a face-to-face interview. Once you've scored an interview, the process really starts.

13. Always remember, to follow up all interviews with an emailed or traditionally mailed thank-you letter.

14. When you receive an offer in hand, make sure you get it in writing.

    Also be sure to request the same amount of vacation time and other benefits you have with your current employer or recent employer.

15. If a bonus is part of the compensation package, make sure you clarify it by asking, "What is the realistic bonus I can expect?"

    Lately, many companies have not been paying bonuses like they did in the past. With any luck, the economy is turning around and you will soon begin to see some type of bonus associated with your new job.


The traditional rule of thumb used to be to expect an offer equal to your most recent salary. Unfortunately, this labor market is different from all other labor markets I have seen professionally over the past 23 years. In some ways, therefore, all bets are off. Welcome to "The New Economy."

Nowadays, a better mantra is: "A bird in the hand is worth two in the bush." In other words, if you like the job, you are going to be gainfully employed, and the commute is reasonable, take the job. If the compensation is not really what you want, so be it. In this tight labor market, it is better to be employed than unemployed.

Given this current labor market, it is not uncommon for people to not have seen any raises for three to four years, to be unemployed for 12 to 18 months, or to be willing to take 50% pay cuts to get back in the game. You need to be practical for the sake of both your career and your family.

Once you've accepted the position, if possible stay with it for a year. Then take time to re-evaluate the situation. As the economy improves, some companies may reward those employees who were realistic about the down business climate.

The labor market is improving. And along with it, national compensation levels will re-stabilize eventually. That will most likely take three to four years until we regain the market levels we saw prior to this deep recession that we're slowly pulling out of.

**CONCLUSION:** If armed with the right job search strategy for their situation, I genuinely believe everyone can find a job. Perseverance, hard work, doing your homework, and great follow-up really make the difference! Congratulations on a successful job search and getting closer to your new job!

## Job Search Expert Action Plan

1  Go to my website to access your book Bonus Material for readers: www.thejobsearchexperts.com/book-readers-bonus-materials/. Save this file as "New Rules—Book Bonus Material" on your desktop (for easy access).

2  Go to your local office products store or retailer and purchase, a 1.5 inch 3-ring binder with a front clear outside pocket sleeve ("view"), one red pen, a package of yellow highlighters (studies have shown that the brain

absorbs better anything on yellow paper or highlighted in yellow) and two 8-tab page divider packages.

3 Print the material you have downloaded onto your desktop, and place it into your Job Search Expert Binder. Separate each chapter with its own tab. Label the spine of your binder: "Job Search Expert Binder."

4 Visit www.thejobsearchexperts.com/my-resume-agent/ to look at "myResume Agent" in more detail. Hint: When you purchase this product, cast you net wide. This is one of the few times I would ever advise submitting your resume to a large number of recruiters.

Choose only recruiters on the list where your past or current professional background matches their recruiting specialty. This product is reasonably priced.

One email blast to the recruiters is included with your purchase of the product. (I have created a partnership with Kennedy Publications to offer you this product.)

# CHAPTER 2

# How to Keep a Positive Mindset in Challenging Times!

*Attitude is the first quality that marks the successful man. If he has a positive attitude and is a positive thinker, who likes challenges and difficult situations, then he has half his success achieved. On the other hand, if he is a negative thinker who is narrow-minded and refuses to accept new ideas and has a defeatist attitude, he hasn't got a chance.*

—LOWELL PEACOCK

LOOKING FOR A NEW JOB is definitely considered a major life change. Most people find searching for new employment to be a turbulent period in their life. Going through a job search is one big emotional roller coaster. In this chapter, I'm going to talk specifically about stress, depression, fear, and how to manage your different emotions to create a stronger attitude and positive mindset!

One thing that seems to be present throughout the job search is stress. Understand that this tendency for stress is a natural one. Stress always comes with change.

## Secrets to Conquering Stress and Fear

When Dr. Arthur Nielsen spoke at Northwestern University on "Managing Economic Stress on the Home Front," his lecture addressed a study conducted by the American Psychological Association. Titled "Stress in America," this research showed how the entire country was coping with this deep recession.

Those individuals involved with the study discovered the following depressive symptoms in response to the stalled economy:

- Feeling depressed or sad: 34%
- Feeling as though they could cry: 32%
- Lack of interest, motivation, or energy: 40%
- Fatigue: 43%
- Insomnia: 47%
- Irritability or anger: 45%

Be careful if you see yourself in one or more of these categories. Depression leads to inactivity, which in turn leads to more depression.

### Stress

When it comes to the best ways to deal with stress, the first thing you must do is be willing to admit that you are enduring stress. I know that I personally try to avoid admitting when I am feeling stressed out. In my mind, confessing stress is a sign of weakness. In reality, the strength arises when you can admit that you're stressed and can back away from the situation and deal with it.

Here are some proven techniques that will help to lessen your job-related stress. Michael McCullough and his colleagues at the University of Miami came up with the following proven procedures. I have taken the liberty of modifying these techniques to tailor them specifically to the job search process.

Begin by thinking about the actual benefits that have come forth as a result of the seemingly negative situation of being laid off and unemployed.

Have these events helped you:

1. Grow stronger or become aware of personal and professional strengths that you were unaware of before?

2. Appreciate certain parts of your life more than before?

3. Become a wiser person about life and yourself?

4. Become better at expressing your feelings and professional goals?

5. Develop into a more compassionate, empathetic, sensitive, and forgiving person?

6. Identify any of your own shortcomings that may be standing in the way of your happiness and next career goals?

Some simple activities that will help when you are stressed:

1. Religion

2. Literature, theater, movies, television

3. Playing or watching sports

4. Hobbies, recreation, travel, and volunteer work

Research has shown that you can reduce your stress by praying for others. Neil Krause at the University of Michigan conducted a study that showed that over 1,000 people who prayed for others helped reduce the financial stresses and strains on the person they were praying for. In the process, they also improved their own overall well-being. It's important to note that praying for material things did not have this same positive effect.

Leisure activities can also have a positive impact on stress. Examining various groups of people following a stressful situation, Sky Chafin at the University of California studied which types of music were better at reducing their blood pressure.

They found that people who listened to Pachelbel's Canon and Vivaldi's Four Seasons Spring, movement 1, relaxed more quickly and their blood pressure dropped more swiftly to its normal level following a stressful event than those who listened to pop or jazz music. In fact, those individuals who listened to pop or jazz following their stressful event had results similar to sitting in total silence. Based on this research, I suggest you go to your local library this week and take out Pachelbel's Canon and Vivaldi's Four Seasons Spring, movement 1.

Another technique worth trying is to spend 30 minutes outside in the sun. With the higher temperature and barometric pressure, you'll find yourself in a better mood and with improved memory. Those who spend less than the suggested "magic" half hour in the sun will discover themselves in a poorer mood than usual. This recommendation is based on a study conducted by Matthew Keller at the Virginia Institute for Psychiatric and Behavioral Genetics.

Another way to relieve stress is to just lighten up! It is suggested that everyone should laugh at least 15 minutes per day. In fact, doing so could save your life. People who are able to spontaneously use humor to help them cope with their stress will have especially healthy immune systems. They are also 40% less likely to suffer a heart attack or stroke, and on average, they live 4.5 years longer than their humorless counterparts. All of these benefits were discovered by Michael Miller and his colleagues in 2005 at the University of Maryland while researching the topic.

To better endure stress, consider adding a canine to your family. People who own dogs tend to cope with stress better than non-dog owners. (That includes us cat owners.) In one study conducted by Erika Friedman at the University of Maryland, dog owners tended to be more relaxed about life, had high self-esteem, and were less likely to be diagnosed with depression.

The primary point of this research was to uncover the social benefit of owning a dog and the positive affect such ownership has on cardiovascular functioning. The results stand to reason.

Dogs have to be walked. Therefore, people who walk dogs tend to interact with other people during such walks. Dogs help promote social contact, which reduces the stress in their owner's lives.

Now the good news is, if you want to embrace this idea and do not own a dog, then you can buy an iDog and still get some of the companionship benefits that help eliminate loneliness. (Marian Banks and colleagues at Saint Louis University School of Medicine conducted a study that substantiated this theory.)

Watching TV can also be a stress buster, depending on what you're watching. If you want to reduce your heart rate and blood pressure in less than a minute, take a break and watch Animal Planet or an animal video. If you watch a soap opera, on the other hand, it produces the same benefits as looking at a blank TV (i.e., virtually none). (Deborah Well, from Queens University in Belfast, found this tendency to be true in her research.)

## Managing the Ups and Downs of the Job Search

One of the things that will help you to develop a positive mindset about your job search is to start feeling more in control. You also need to face up to how frightened and angry you are if you are currently unemployed, especially in a challenging economy like this one.

You may also be dealing with feelings such as fear, anger, shock, disbelief, self-doubt, denial, betrayal, guilt, depression, shame, etc. over losing your job. First off, let me say that all of these responses are normal and common. Unfortunately, everybody goes through them at various times while looking for a new job. They are normal emotional stages everyone deals with.

Do not worry if at times you feel discouraged or emotionally out of control. Traditionally, when you're unemployed, the five main emotions are anger or being mad, sadness, shame, fear, and gladness. (Why gladness? A lot of people are relieved to be free of the jobs they were unhappy in.)

Denial is also part of the game. One day you'll find yourself feeling up and the next day down in the dumps. Your response to your situation is bound to be a roller coaster of emotional mood swings. Again, this is normal. You are not losing your mind!

The trick is to manage these emotions and compartmentalize them. This way, they do not paralyze you from taking action to regain control of your life and find a great job you can be excited about! *The longer you allow these emotions to bring you down and paralyze you, the longer it will take you to land your ideal job.*

Ironically, it is when you might be most discouraged with your job search progress that you most need your determination and confidence to come out of the situation. They are what will position you as a winner. I suggest you go to my blog, on the web site www.TheJobSearchExperts.com: "Sweet Job Advice." In particular, read the December 15, 2010 entry, the bamboo story from Zig Ziglar.

This story drives home the important point that a job search is similar to growing a bamboo tree. Both a bamboo tree and a job search take a lot of preparation, feeding (your pipeline), and nurturing (follow through) before the fruits of your efforts are necessarily seen.

The key is to keep watering and taking care of your bamboo tree. Suddenly, after five years of not "growing," your bamboo tree will grow 90 feet in one season! The same is true for your job search: Suddenly, after all your efforts, you will be rewarded with interviews and job offers.

It will not help your situation to continuously beat up on yourself, though we all have done so at one time or another. Being hard on ourselves is human nature in terms of how we cope with such situations.

If you find yourself going through a temporary phase of being completely overwhelmed with your job search, take some time off. You'll need a break to get re-energized and shake off the negative thinking.

If you're looking full time for a job, I suggest you take three hours off a week. Reward yourself by doing something that you normally would not have had the luxury of doing while you were working. It could be volunteering at your children's school, meeting a friend for breakfast or lunch, etc.

Allow yourself an hour to walk outside the house. Another idea is to engage in some type of physical activity, such as a house maintenance project. (Your spouse will be pleased. Don't forget that this period of instability is a particularly hard time for spouses as well.) Try to find some project you can easily control, complete, and witness visual results from.

I personally love gardening. I remember being depressed following the death of my mother. The day after the funeral, I felt overwhelmed. So I basically went out into the garden and the hillside and probably chopped down about 25 buckthorn trees. The physical labor and visual results helped me refocus and get re-energized.

If the weather is bad, you can also work inside the house, touching up some of the chipped paint or caulk or repainting a room, closet, basement, or garage.

Some of the typical types of emotions you might experience or go through during your job search are the following:

- Shock
- Denial
- Betrayal
- Anger
- Isolation
- Sadness
- Depression
- Shame
- Fear

Relative to the situation, fear, to me, can be the most paralyzing and insidious of all these emotions. You need to manage any fear you have or it will manage you and try to destroy your spirit. One of the ways to manage your fear is to push through it by being grateful for what you have. When you practice gratitude, you dissipate and weaken the fear. You are then in control of the fear instead of the other way around.

Fear → Gratitude → Happiness

One of the most important techniques for boosting happiness revolves around the psychology of gratitude. Psychologists Robert Emmons and Michael McCullough performed a study with three groups of people to test this theory. One group wrote about five things that annoyed them, another group wrote about five things that took place the previous week, and the third group wrote about the five things they were grateful for each week. The last group, the ones who wrote about what they were grateful for, were, in the end, happier, much more optimistic about the future, and physically healthier. They even exercised more.

I am now going to suggest my own personal spin on this method, which is to name five things, first thing in the morning before you get out of bed, that you are grateful for. Repeat this process right before you go to bed, naming five things you were grateful for during that day.

If you have the time, write these gratitude items down on the front of a 3 x 5″ card each morning and on the back of the card at end of each day. If you do so, it will really strengthen the process for you. I'm a firm believer that writing something down and verbalizing it is stronger than just thinking about it.

Another somewhat-related trick is to replay the day's events in your head. If something did not go the way you wanted it to, replay the event in your mind. As you do so, rewrite the story to reflect a positive turn of events. Do this right before you go to sleep. It's always better to go to bed with positive thoughts lingering as opposed to negative ones. To overcome them, you must keep pushing the negative thoughts back.

I know everyone is telling you that what you're currently going through is for the best, and there is a reason behind your unemployment. I also know that does not make it any easier. In the over 23 years that I've helped people find new jobs, I have seen this tendency hold true the majority of the time.

In *Think and Grow Rich,* Napoleon Hill said, "Every negative event contains within it the seed of an equal or greater benefit." I believe that with all my heart, even if we may not know what that reason is right now.

Another way to look at it would be from Mary Kay Ash's viewpoint: "For every failure, there's an alternative course of action. You just have to find it. When you come to a roadblock, take a detour."

When you start feeling down, remember that the "no" you just got from one company or hiring authority puts you that much closer to the "yes" and the job offer that's waiting for you.

### Secrets to Increasing Belief in Yourself

You must feel the confidence in your strength and personal power to take ownership of your career and your life. Ironically enough, most job seekers have a tendency not to reach out to others during this time. In fact, it's a time when they least feel like reaching out. However, it is important to make that effort now and not isolate yourself. Reaching out to others will help keep your demons at bay.

Join a local career support group, a church support group, a networking group, or a job mastermind group. Ideally, your group should be made up of four to five people with everyone being accountable to one another. Studies show that the job seekers who are involved with some type of support group secure employment faster.

Another way to enhance your self-belief is to attend my Job Search Experts teleseminars or coaching sessions. If you're not able to attend the live sessions, we can send you an audio replay.

Regardless of how you choose to reach out, you must be committed to your outcome. You must be determined to let nothing stand in your way. Assess what type of self-limiting beliefs are holding you back and sabotaging your job search.

I'm going to suggest that you go to your local library and get a copy of the book, CD, or DVD, *The Secret* by Rhonda Bryne. These media contain some wonderful examples of the law of attraction. *The Secret* personally inspired me during a particularly tough time following the death of my mother.

The law of attraction works this way: You get what you focus on and believe in, provided you are committed to taking action. There is also *The Power*, another book similar to *The Secret* by the same author. While you're there, check your library for other outstanding motivational books for additional possible readings.

If you're of the male persuasion, you may need a little extra help in this department. That's because men's self-worth/self-esteem is traditionally tied more to their professional career than women's. Guys tend to be harder hit by the loss of their job and less likely to reach out for help. Remember that you must reach out.

As Henry Ford once said, "Whether you think you can or think you can't . . . you're right."

In essence, we're really all responsible for our own destiny. No one else is; you are! It's up to you to drive this ship. You and you alone are responsible for finding that next great job. In this new economy, the more direct ownership you take of the job search process, the faster you'll land your next great job!

### Tips on Managing the Fear and Uncertainty

During your job search, you'll be challenged by many feelings, such as fear, worry, and uncertainty. You'll find yourself in a constant struggle with yourself over having a good mental attitude. You're basically on a mental battlefield that must be won if your life is to be filled with abundance (i.e., finding the right job).

To emerge the victor, you must establish and maintain confidence in both yourself and your ability to successfully find a new job. Confidence is the most important factor in protecting yourself from the negativity of the job search ups and downs. When you lack confidence, fear and worry will take control. Your job search progress will be held captive and your momentum will grind to a complete halt.

This is when you have to push the fear aside and regain your confidence level. One of the easiest techniques for accomplishing this, as I've alluded to earlier, is to spend five minutes thinking about what you're grateful for in your life (e.g., your children, your family members, the beautiful sky outside, the wonderful weather, etc.). Taking the time to remind yourself of the simple abundance that currently exists in your life will help stamp out all the negative forces that are bringing you down.

## Gratitude Rock

Another confidence-building technique is to carry a gratitude rock with you in your right pocket (or left pocket if you happen to be left-handed). Every time you feel any fear or doubt, reach into your pocket and touch the rock. By touching it, you refocus on the positive aspects of your life that you're grateful for. As a result, going forward you will find yourself redirected and strong.

Fear breeds doubt and doubt leads to a loss of confidence. It then becomes a vicious cycle. If left unchecked, you will begin a downward spiral that will continue to gain momentum. Suddenly life is overwhelming, and you feel like it's out of control. This sensation will bring you to an immediate standstill, freezing you from an effective job search. It also puts a tremendous drain on your energy.

You have the choice to either:

1. Play the denial game, or

2. Go into limbo, or

3. Choose to confront the issue head on by stepping into and managing the fear.

When you confront the fear, you can focus on the immediate situation and get back to working on your job search.

Fear drains the energy you need for your job search. If you want to gain confidence, work on your job search, and restore your energy to maximum level, then you must first confront your fear.

George Addair runs workshops titled "The Road to Freedom Paradigm." His philosophy is: Everything you want is on the other side of fear. To overcome fear, you must have faith in the outcome.

To rise above your fears and uncertainties, you need to start rebuilding your confidence. Initial steps you should take to do so include:

1. Resolving any unfinished business you may have that is draining your energy—Work on redirecting current negative energy away from your life.

2. Identifying your deeper fears

Schedule some quiet time by yourself to think about:

1. What do you fear most?

2. What do you fear in the future?

3. What do you fear right now?

Sometimes without realizing it, we can sabotage our results. Reflective thinking in answering these questions should give you clarity. Once you have clearly identified your fears, you have a tremendous advantage. Now you can design strategies to combat the fears whenever they start creeping up.

Each time one of your fears comes up, start asking yourself the question, "What can I do to overcome this?" You now have a strategic plan to counteract your fear, which will not only help increase your confidence and certainty but also give you a feeling of being back in control. You are taking "the bull by the horns."

Hold on to your confidence at the height of your fear. Times like this can be one of life's greatest challenges. With your newfound strength, expect to do well, no matter what situation you're facing.

Manage and conquer your fear. Everything you want is on the other side of fear.

When you are able to keep your fear at bay, you'll leave behind the majority of your worry and guilt. You'll then notice a renewed sense of energy.

Understand that confidence grows by doing, not thinking. You need to assess whether what you're doing for your job search is giving you the results you want. You need to ask yourself, "Is there something I should be changing?" Sometimes change is difficult but necessary. Also understand that procrastination is a way of staying stuck. It keeps you from driving your job search campaign. Remember to take action on a daily basis.

What action are you going to take today that will have a positive impact on your job search?

Now is the time to embrace change—change regarding yourself, change regarding how you are approaching yourself, change regarding how you're approaching your job search. Take a second look and explore any additional unique talents you may have that you're not communicating or utilizing at this time that could assist you in getting closer to your goal.

Take one day at a time, make one decision at a time, and accomplish one result at a time.

Confidence comes from combining a positive attitude with positive action. You are in control of both of these aspects of your life. Every day you have the choice to think more positively. You also have the choice to take positive action or not. There is a direct link between your attitude and the choices you ultimately make.

### How to Create More Optimism While in Your Job Search

I have, fortunately, been one of those people for whom the glass is half full. If you are someone who, by nature, sees the glass as half empty, then you will need to work on trying to change your approach to life. Strive to add more optimism to your mindset and outlook. I can guarantee it will do wonders for your job search.

Alan Loy McGinnis, author and therapist, shares the following twelve characteristics of an optimist in his book *The Power of Optimism*:

1. Optimists are seldom surprised by trouble.

2. Optimists do not look for partial solutions.

3. Optimists believe they have control over their futures and are not just victims of circumstances.

4. Optimists interrupt their negative trains of thought.

5. Optimists heighten their powers of appreciation.

6. Optimists use their imaginations to rehearse success.

7. Optimists are cheerful even when they cannot be happy.

8. Optimists believe they have an almost unlimited capacity for stretching.

9. Optimists build lots of love into their lives.

10. Optimists like to swap good news.

11. Optimists accept what cannot be changed.

12. Optimists usually allow for regular physical and mental renewal.

McGinnis tells us that studies show optimists excel in school, have better health, make more money, establish long and happy marriages, stay connected to their children, and perhaps even live longer.

What are you waiting for?!

## Secrets to Strengthening Attitude and Confidence in Challenging Moments

A job search is always challenging, but it's particularly challenging when one is unemployed. At times, life can seem like a roller coaster ride. Some days you will feel better than others. Some days will be more productive than others. But as Scarlett O'Hara said in *Gone with the Wind*, "Tomorrow is another day." Start each day with fresh confidence and strength of heart.

> *The winners in life think constantly in terms of I can, I will, and I am. Losers, on the other hand, concentrate their waking thoughts on what they should have or would have done, or what they can't do.*
> —Dr. Dennis Waitley, *The Psychology of Winning*

I want to share with you some other ideas you can use to help keep a positive mindset in the midst of the job search ups and downs.

The first is to embrace the six confidence-building strategies suggested by Jack Canfield, Mark Victor Hansen, and Les Hewitt in *The Power of Focus*:

1. Every day, remind yourself that you did something well.

2. Read inspiring biographies and autobiographies.

3. Be thankful.

4. Build excellent support around you.

5. Push yourself to accomplish short-term goals.

6. Do something for yourself every week.

The road to confidence is paved with weekly victories. Learn to applaud them.

Jack Canfield, Mark Victor Hansen and Les Hewitt have graciously allowed me to share this with you. You will find the subject more in depth in their book.

The key to maintaining a positive mindset during your job search is being prepared to keep getting back on your horse. Sit straight in your saddle with confidence.

- Acknowledge your stress.
- Acknowledge your different emotions at different times.
- Define your fears.
- Define what you are grateful for.
- Admit when you are overwhelmed and address the situation.
- Maintain your confidence, happiness, and strength of heart at all possible times.
- Rely on your loved ones and your support system of friends.
- Rely on a higher authority to help you through the rough spots.
- Never give up on the belief in yourself and that you will succeed in finding the right job.

Remember to:

1. Put things in perspective. Look beyond the present.

2. Make sure you are reaching out for support.

3. Remind yourself that this is only a small portion of your life's big picture.

4. Continue to look for a job. Set goals and keep working at it.

I believe in you. I know you will find your next great job. Stay in the game. You will need determination, patience, and a committed drive to keep pressing forward toward your goal.

*The mind can convince a competent person that
he is incompetent or an adequate person that he is highly
talented. Unfortunately, self-doubt and negative attitudes
seem to have a more powerful influence on the mind than
positive attitudes. Usually a person is not aware that he
is setting himself up or limiting his capabilities.*
—Bruce Bowman

It is up to you to decide how you want to live each day. What are you going to do with each day of our life?

*You are in the driver's seat of your life and can point your life down any road you want to travel. You can go as fast or as slow as you want to go . . . and you can change the road you're on at any time.*
—Jinger Heath

## Job Search Expert Action Plan

1 Find a picture of something you love, are passionate about, or represents a goal. Print a copy and insert it into the front outside cover of your Job Search Expert Binder as an inspiration. This image can be a picture of your loved ones, partner, pet, sports car, boat, sunset, favorite quote, or prayer. The only ground rule is that it must be something you will enjoy looking at. It should be something that will act as an inspirational vision to keep you motivated to press forward with your job search and land that next great job.

2 Read your Bonus Material, "The Sweet Success of Persistence."

3 Find a local support group to participate in on a weekly basis, preferably face to face.

**Additional Job Search Notes**

# PART 2

# Job Search
# Success Tools

# CHAPTER 3

# Secrets to a Homerun
# with Your Resume

*We judge ourselves by what
we feel capable of doing, while
others judge us by what we
have already done.*

—HENRY WADSWORTH LONGFELLOW

BEFORE DIVING INTO some of the ways you can make sure you're differentiating yourself with your resume, let's briefly discuss some resume basics.

*Basic Statistics in Today's Market*
- On average, your resume will be *looked at for only 10 seconds!!*
- The average person in today's labor market is in a job for only 2.5 to 3 years.
- After graduating from college, most people can expect to have 12 to 16 jobs in their lifetime.

*Purposes of Your Resume*

1. Your resume serves as a marketing tool. It acts as your marketing "brochure" to pique hirers' interest enough to call you in for an interview. Your resume has been sent in advance, as part of your "job solicitation," in response to an ad, a posting, a networking lead, or a cold call.

2. Your resume helps guide the interview process.

3. Your resume represents your background when you are not physically present. After the interview, your resume has, most likely, been left behind for others to read.

## Mechanics and Actual Technical Resume Advice

We've already discussed how to leverage Microsoft Excel in the job search process. Now, let's turn our attention to using some additional job search tools available in Microsoft Word. Don't forget that you can get resume templates online. Simply visit Microsoft Resume Templates (www.office.microsoft.com/en-us/templates/CT010104337.aspx). You should be able to download them for free. Alternatively, on your computer, go to Microsoft Word and click on:

- File
- New
- Templates or New from Template

Then click on either Templates on Office Online or Templates on My Computer, Other Documents, where you will find four resume templates.

To find these resume templates online, you can also Google and enter "Microsoft Online Resume Templates" into the search bar.

In the new Windows 2010, you will find 44 new templates supplied courtesy of Monster.com. In addition, Windows 2010 by Microsoft is giving you 119 basic resumes, 108 job-specific resumes, and 22 situation-specific resumes (mostly for high school graduates and very specific situations like someone wanting to relocate).

When you get your resume printed, I suggest an Ariel, Verdana, or Times New Roman font in a 12-point size using heavy linen, brilliant white, 24-lb. paper. Keep ¾ to one-inch margins all around.

### 7 Styles of Resumes You Need to Be Aware Of

There are basically seven types of resume forms from which you can choose. You will most likely select the one that best suits your style, with the understanding that in certain unique situations, you may want turn to some of the other alternatives.

1. Reverse chronological (preferred one)

2. Combination type, both chronological and functional

3. Functional

4. Biographical letter (the "no resume" resume)

5. "Handbill" resume and mini resume

6. "Tell-all" resume

7. Targeted resume

Let's take a look at each one of these options individually.

### Reverse Chronological

1. Reverse chronological is the most preferred and popular type of resume. I have to tell you that after over 17 years of looking at approximately 43,000+ resumes, this is still the one I personally prefer.

Why? Because it is easy to quickly get a sense of what the job applicant has been doing in their most recent positions.

## Combination Type: Chronological and Functional

2. The combination type of chronological and functional resume hybrid is frequently used when someone has had a number of promotions within in the same company. If you were to choose this type of resume, you would list your accomplishments, skills, and experience first by functional area of expertise. Next, you would list your employment history.

This is a resume that works well when you're customizing your qualifications to a specific job. What makes the combination resume ideal for this type of situation is that you can highlight your skills that are relevant to the particular job you are applying for at the top, where they're most likely to be noticed.

## Functional

3. A functional resume puts the reader's focus on your accomplishments, skills, and experience rather than your chronological work history. This type of resume works well if you are in the midst of a major career change or if you have some time gaps in your work history.

## Biographical

4. The biographical resume is just like it sounds. Basically, it's a biographical letter that highlights your career contributions. Frankly speaking, I find this type of resume hard to read, simply because it asks the reader to plod through a format that is not quickly and easily digestible in today's fast-paced world that prefers to move in sound bites.

## Handbill

5. The handbill resume and mini resume, if not identical, are very similar to one another. This type of resume is a one-page summary or shorter version of your full qualifications. It kind of reminds me of the five-minute date idea. What I like about this resume option is that in some situations it can basically serve

as a "tease" to get you to the next level in the hiring process. Sometimes less is better.

### Tell-All Resume

6. The tell-all resume is another one that lives up to its name. It can be as long as 10 pages. In a nutshell, job applicants tell everything they have professionally accomplished within these pages.

You will tend to see this length of resume later on in the interviewing process. It is also used a lot by people in the academic world, people with patents, and individuals with professional research articles to their credit. This type of resume will most likely get you screened out of the job search game early if you present it right out of the starting gate. Remember that when it comes to the length of your resume, less is better initially.

### Target Resume

7. We've already touched on the target resume. This type of resume is customized to a specific job. It highlights the experience and skills that are most relevant to the position to which you're applying. To gain a leg up, customize your resume's keywords to the job posting's keywords.

The choice is ultimately yours, but when all is all said and done, I still prefer the chronological resume over the other options.

### The Reader of Your Resume

When creating your resume, remember that studies show the typical reader will spend less than 10 seconds scanning it. As they glance at it, they are looking for a reason to put it in their "A," "B," or "C" piles.

If your resume lands in the "A" pile, it means that something has caught the reader's eye enough that they plan on looking at it in more detail later on. A spot in the "B" pile usually means you've attracted moderate interest, while a "C" pile resume is getting pretty close to being tossed in the trash can.

How do we get a resume that will wind up in the "A" pile, stay there all the way through the hiring process, and ultimately rise to the top?

### "Accomplishments" Are the Name of the Game—How You Land the Job!

If you want to earn a spot in the coveted "A" list, you have to make sure you've created a powerful, accomplishment-oriented resume with a strong cover letter that acts as a marketing tool.

In a resume you are, in essence, "marketing" yourself. You are the product you want to sell. That being said, the more strongly you describe your accomplishments, skills, and experience the more likely you will be called in for an interview and get the job offer.

Never forget that your accomplishments are the backbone of your resume. They communicate your professional strengths and your ability to make a positive difference not only to an organization but also, more importantly, their bottom line.

Accomplishment statements should be short, measureable (quantifiable), and results-oriented. When writing them, you should use vivid, descriptive action words. Such an approach will help create a word picture in the hiring authority's mind. When you use action verbs, you enable the prospective employer to visualize you accomplishing the important tasks you've highlighted with your previous employers. You then give the hiring authority the impression that you can accomplish the same results for their organization.

You want to make sure you're using powerful action verbs at the beginning of all your accomplishment bullets. You should also work at coming up with phrases other than "Responsible for . . ." and "Worked with . . . ," only because a lot of people use them. As a result, many hiring authorities have become immune to the impact of those types of phrasings.

Suggested alternatives:

- Captivated
- Championed
- Directed
- Exceeded
- Pioneered
- Formulized
- Formulated
- Generated
- Intensified
- Leveraged
- Masterminded
- Maximized
- Mentored
- Optimized
- Orchestrated
- Re-engineered
- Spearheaded
- Structured
- Proliferated
- Recaptured
- Regained
- Rejuvenated

Refer to your synonym feature in Microsoft Word or to www.thesaurus.com for more options.

I'd like to share with you some additional guidelines to keep in mind when playing up your accomplishments:

1. If possible, use present/active tense, not passive tense. The result will be that you accomplishments sound stronger.

2. Use adjectives and adverbs as little as possible.

3. When using nouns, make sure they are as specific and descriptive as possible.

4. Always pick the larger but still believable number. For example, if you have a choice between $5,000 and 25%, use 25%.

5. This is so important that it bears emphasis: USE NUMBERS, actual numbers, $ signs, and % signs. The human eye is visually drawn, by instinct, into that area of the paper. Quantify your accomplishments whenever possible.

6. Proofread all your verbs and nouns for agreement, tense, and correct usage.

Your accomplishments will fall into one of two categories. They will be either process-oriented or project-oriented.

Process-oriented accomplishments show how you have successfully managed a problematic situation over a period of time. They indicate that you are used to facilitating stable situations and systems. By highlighting them, you are communicating your ability to solve problems for your prospective employer.

Project-oriented accomplishments, on the other hand, show that you are the type of individual who will get projects done. They indicate that you can solve any problems that arise in projects that are assigned to you. Such accomplishments will communicate the problems you were faced with, your solutions to those problems, and the overall impact. They will also emphasize the solutions to those particular situations and how those resolutions impacted the organization. This is similar to a SAR (Situation, Action, and Result) interviewing question and answer, in this case on your resume.

### Nuts and Bolts

Now that we've covered the basics, let's get down to some of the nuts and bolts of creating a powerful resume.

You should take the time to create three to four accomplishments for each job you've held throughout your career. Complete this same process for any volunteer activities you've been involved in. Save this document as a research file. Later, you will draw off it when creating your customized resumes. Label your document "ALL Accomplishments."

This file will become your resource library. You will consult it not only in devising your customized resumes but also for your cover letters, follow-up letters, and informational interviews.

Remember that the goal here is to create a powerful resume that will compel people to contact you for an interview. That's when the process has really started!

## Summary Section

Try using a "Summary" section at the top of your resume. This opening strategy is a great way to try and "position" yourself. Here is where you can show your prospective employers why you're different from all the other candidates. It's here where you showcase your abilities, experience, and personality.

Customize this area for your different target companies. One good way of doing this is to underline and bold the sections you want readers to focus on. Then in your resume, you can also underline and bold the sections that apply to the points you lured them to in your "Summary."

In your "Summary," highlight the skills and qualities you've uncovered in your research that the company is specifically seeking. Here is where you position yourself and reveal to your prospective employers the most important things you want them to know about you.

## 19 Secrets to a Powerful Resume

1. For the most part, focus on the last 10 to 15 years of employment.

2. In this current job market, avoid using a "Job Objective" section. Currently, the odds are that it will be used to screen you out as opposed to escorting you in.

3. Consider changing your past job titles if they do not truly represent what you were doing. Use the more traditional titles currently being used in the marketplace for your areas of expertise. Generally speaking, a title that was unique to one organization but is not recognized by the overall market could be screening you out of the hiring process.

4. Include a Summary Statement. This is where you differentiate yourself from the other candidates who are

applying for the same position. Consider underlining or bolding the most important phrases here to easily get your message noticed by the reader.

5. After creating a list of about seven to eight accomplishments per job, go back and rank them in order of strength. Create an "A" group for those achievements where you contributed a lot to the company, a "B" group for those where, quantitatively speaking, you did not contribute quite as much, and a "C" group for those activities that were required of you but were not as critical to your employer's success. This last group could also include results you started to achieve but did not get a chance to see through to completion prior to leaving the organization you were working for.

6. Keep some of your accomplishments general in nature. This approach will help the reader of your resume easily transfer and apply your message to his or her organization. You do not want your accomplishments to be so company- or industry-specific that they become too niche-oriented to the non-competing and non-industry jobs you are considering.

7. Keep your accomplishments brief and specific. Whenever possible, make sure you communicate their financial impact in terms of concrete dollars, numbers, or percent. The human eyes is always pulled to seeing quantifiable symbols (e.g., $, #, or %). Make your achievements quantitative whenever possible.

8. Put the quantifiable information at the beginning of the bullet rather than in the middle or at the end.

9. Stack your most impressive quantifiable accomplishments at the top of the list.

10. Tell the reader how you saved your employer money, increased the company's market share, improved corporate productivity, resolved problems, created solutions, attained something for the first time, made life easier, etc. Specify how you impacted the business's bottom line!

11. Make sure the reader of your resume can see how you recognized an opportunity or problem and then acted to solve it. Organizations are looking for problem solvers, particularly in this economy. Focus on results (i.e., what effect did your actions have in your past organization).

12. Another way to look at creating your accomplishment bullets is with this equation: Responsibilities + Situation + Action = Results.

13. Keep in mind, the more details you supply the more powerful your resume will be (provided you do not ramble on with an excessive amount of details).

14. Go with a **results**-oriented resume. It is always more powerful than one that addresses only responsibilities.

15. Keep it simple and straightforward. Less is more. In particular, less narrative is more powerful. Think of it as a first date; you want to whet the hiring authorities' appetite for what's to come. You don't want to tell or show them everything in your first correspondence. Treat it as you would a "first date."

16. Do not bog down your reader with jargon and abbreviations that are unique to your industry and that they may not understand. That is one of the fastest ways to get screened out of a potential job.

17. Your resume must be easy to scan. Pick 15 to 20 keywords or phrases for your job expertise and industry

and incorporate them into your resume in a way that they're easy to scan.

18. Make sure you start the top of page 2 with something important. If someone goes to the second page, they will start at the top.

19. Always use accurate information. Do not grossly misrepresent your personal or professional information.

## 5 Special Resume Tips for the "Over 45" Crowd

The goal is to have the movers and shakers who are reading your resume focus on your accomplishments and what you bring to the party. You don't want them to get hung up on your age.

To ensure that doesn't happen, follow this advice:

1. In some cases, it would be advisable to remove any age-specific references from your resume. A good example of this is to leave off the year of your college graduation under "Education." Instead, just list the name of the school and your major (assuming it is applicable to the job you are applying for).

2. Consider removing your work history prior to 1990 or so. The only time you should ignore this advice is when something you accomplished a long time ago is particularly relevant to the specific job you are applying for now (e.g., competitive product background).

3. Be careful how you word your professional tenure. Instead of saying, ". . . 25 years in the industry," you could say, ". . . with over 15 years of experience."

4. Whenever possible, use names of companies that still exist or use their new name [e.g., GE Lamp (old), versus GE Lighting (current)]. Also, use your former employer's current company name if that company was bought or sold in the past.

5. Make sure you highlight any new skills you've acquired, particularly in the high-tech area.

## Overall Recap

Initially, spend most of your time building your accomplishment list. Then focus on creating a quality "Summary" that will successfully position you for the type of job you want to interview for. At the same time, differentiate yourself from the other job candidates who are vying for the same position.

Set a timer for 10 seconds and conduct a mock pre-interview with a friend. When the timer goes off, have your friend tell you what they know about you and your professional background based on reading/scanning your resume for 10 to 15 seconds.

If you are not happy with their answer, look at your resume and try to figure out where you message is breaking down.

Bear in mind that 90% of people finding jobs are currently succeeding through networking. Keep working on your list of 200 target companies. In your research, you will uncover what traits and qualities they are looking for in an employee. That is precisely the information you need to customize in your resume, cover letters, and follow-up letters to them.

Remember in your initial contact with a company to send a two-page customized resume that is detailed but brief. You want to entice the hiring authority into asking for additional information. That will necessitate him or her having to reach out to you to set up an interview.

Save your long, full resume for your second face-to-face interview. After you have completed your first interview, you will have a better idea of how to customize your resume to address the company's specific needs.

This is Marketing 101. Remember that you are the product. Keep doing this method over and over for every target company, and before you know it, you'll have sold yourself.

Before I close this chapter, I would like to leave you with a thought for today . . .

### Capitalize on Your Strengths

*Thomas Alva Edison was almost deaf. But he didn't waste valuable time trying to teach himself to hear. Instead, he concentrated on the things he did best: thinking, organizing, and creating. And he became great because of it.*
—Anonymous

Remember to focus on your strengths. If you have them but the reader cannot understand or see them clearly on your resume, then you will not get the desired results from him or her. You will not make it to first base, never mind home plate!

You must communicate and position yourself as the strong, successful person you are. Hiring authorities need to know and appreciate that you are the best person to improve their organization!

## Job Search Expert Action Plan:

1  To view some templates of different styles of resumes, visit www.office.microsoft.com/en-us/templates/CT010104337 .aspx.

2  Download various templates that you find online and like. Print your favorite ones and put them in your Job Search Expert Binder for Chapter 3: "Resumes."

3  Read over your Bonus Material for this chapter, "Secrets to a Powerful Resume: Accomplishments," three times. Highlight the information in this document you plan to use to help strengthen your resume.

CHAPTER 4

# Powerful Letters That Get Noticed and Read

*Communication does require both effective sending and receiving.*

—ANONYMOUS

## Overview Tips

BECAUSE THIS TOPIC ranked #2 in importance on a survey we conducted at the end of last year, I think it's important to devote some time to job search–related correspondence.

The topic is broad and complex, so we'll devote full coverage of it to future books and seminars. That way, we can break it down more into separate sessions. For the time being, let's take a broader-brush approach to the subject. Later on in this chapter, we'll then delve into some of the mechanics.

Part of your Bonus Material for this chapter will consist of a list of some of the books I researched while coming up with additional material for this chapter. My suggestion is to visit your local library and take out some of the books I'm sharing with you. Then study them at leisure at home. They will arm you with additional ideas of verbiage you can incorporate into your letters. It will be in your best interest to quickly scan several of these books and make photocopies of the best sections from each that work for your particular job search needs.

That's your homework assignment. Now let's get back to the topic at hand. In a survey of 500 employment professionals cited in *The Perfect Cover Letter* by Richard H. Beatty, 76% said that they had eliminated resumes submitted to them on the basis of their being poorly written and/or containing typos or grammatical errors.

Let this be a lesson to you. Your resume and cover letter are often your first introduction to your potential employer. Initially, you will be judged on your written skills and your ability to effectively communicate information regarding your professional background. There's just no way around it.

That being said, in today's market, if your cover letter and resume are not perfect, you will not make the cut to the next level. The hiring authority will simply toss your paperwork in the trash can and that will be that.

After putting all kinds of time and effort into "perfecting" their resume, there is a tendency for some individuals to cut corners on their cover letter. Big mistake!

When all is said and done, you will feel like 90% of your time went into writing your resume and the other 10% into revising and proofing it, but the reality is really the opposite. It typically takes 10% of your time to write and 90% of your time to proof, refine, rework, and customize your resume. The same is true for your job-related letters.

Job seekers will typically fall into one of two categories: those who spend too much time overworking their resumes and those who rush out their resumes with a lot of typos on them.

Some of those who are overworking their resumes are subconsciously stalling in an effort to avoid getting out into the job search jungle. They are uncertain how to go about their job search and they're afraid of being rejected and let down. Most people who are looking for a job have gone through all of these feelings at one time or another.

Make sure you put good, quality time into all your paper-work, both your resumes and your letters. When possible, it is best if you can customize all of your written documents for each situation you encounter. The extra effort will pay off.

Regardless of whether you follow my customization suggestion, this is NOT an area where you want to slack off. It's here where you can differentiate yourself from the rest of the pack and really shine! If you go about this process correctly, it will be the second sales tool working in your benefit. Make an extra effort to show prospective employers why you're the one they need to interview and hire for the position!

Remember, studies show that, on average, a job candidate's paperwork is initially looked at for approximately only 10 seconds. If you are successful and have piqued the hiring authority's interest, they will read your resume more thoroughly. If they remain interested, they will then read your cover letter in its entirety. If the cover letter looks like it will take longer than one minute to read, however, they will be less apt to read through to the end. Your cover letter should give them a general sense of you the person and your personality. It should also help them judge the effectiveness of your communication skills.

### 3 Purposes of Your Cover Letter and 2 Hints

1. A business letter to transmit your resume to a prospective employer

2. A letter of introduction to accompany your resume that introduces you and your professional background to a prospective employer

3. *A sales letter to convince a prospective employer that you have something of value to contribute to their organization—just enough to motivate them to grant you an interview*

You need to remember to write you cover letter for the reader (i.e., your prospective employer) not from your perspective. What is of interest to them? What are they looking for?

Remember that part of the process involves increasing a hiring authority's ability to know, like, and trust you. They also need to be able to quickly obtain some sense of how you can 1) save them money, 2) make them money, and/or 3) solve some problem for them that are currently not getting resolved.

Don't forget to do as much research as possible on the companies you will be sending your cover letter to. The more you know about 1) the organization, 2) the jobs available there, 3) the hiring authority, 4) the company's customer base, and 5) its competitors, the stronger and more targeted your letter will be to your audience, the hiring authority.

Obviously, your research will be more intense for your target group (25 ideal employers) versus your broadcast group (100 to 200 companies worth considering). Still, the primary question is: "What factors will motivate an employer to want to interview me?"

Industry experts tell us that the average reader used to spend 15 seconds looking at the cover letter before they moved on. This number has shrunk with the recession and the increased number of resumes that are being sent out. Keep in mind too that like everyone, the human resource department has seen staffing cuts and, in some cases, is outsourcing this screening process to independent contractors. As a result, it's a good bet that a fair number of resume reviewers will not be well versed with the company's genuine needs.

Perhaps this is why approximately 90% of all job seekers are currently landing their jobs in the hidden job market and through networking. To increase your odds, here are a few hints for getting an interview:

1. Send your paperwork to a high-level executive within the company who works in the particular business function or

discipline most closely related to the position for which you are applying. Try to get it in the hands of a high-ranking individual in the job area that is most appropriate relative to your expertise.

This strategy will increase your odds of tapping into the hidden job market. At this level, these executives might be aware of additional positions that have not yet been officially posted but need to be filled within the organization.

A lot of times, even the HR people are not aware of these future jobs. That being said, if you target high-level executives, your information will likely be given greater consideration than it would be by the overloaded HR department.

2. Cull through your networking contacts and research to unearth the name of an actual person within the organization whom you can actually leverage to refer you. Then, if possible, use the name of that person you have networked with, either internally or externally, in your cover letter.

## 9 Types of Cover Letters You Need for Your Job Search

1. Letter to Company—in response to an ad/lead

2. Letter to Recruiter—in response to an ad/lead

3. Letter to Company—"cold call" * (prospecting letter)

4. Letter to Recruiter—"cold call"

5. Networking Letter—using your networking lead to help land you an interview

6. Referral Letter—using your referral's name in your letter

7. Follow-up Letter/Thank-you Letter to an interviewer or referral

8. Broadcast Letter (without resume) (hidden job market technique)

9. Target Company Letters

### Types of Cover Letter Formats

1. Full Block: 49%

2. Block: 34%

3. Modified Block: 17%

With the Full Block cover letter, everything is left justified. It has a neat, crisp, and easy-to-read appearance. It also tends to look uniform, structured, formal, and businesslike.

With the Block and Modified Block cover letter, you have a similar appearance to the Full Block but not quite as formal and stiff. In my opinion, the Block and Modified Block formats give more the feeling of "person to business" as opposed to the "business to business" feel of the Full Block.

The Block (blocked paragraph with indented return address, date, and complimentary closing and signature lines) cover letter is more a "personal to business" format and not quite as causal as the Modified Block style.

Prior to writing your cover letters, do not forget:

1. Your cover letter should complement your resume, not duplicate it. You should use different language in the two documents.

2. Your cover letter should show a personal side to you in addition to providing an overview of the facts contained in your resume. Use the name of the person you're writing to toward the end of the letter to appear friendly and personal.

3. Perform a self-analysis to assess whether your professional background is relevant and to determine if you're really

interested in working for this company and within the geographical location listed at this time.

4. Get as much information about the position you are applying for as you can. Ideally these details would include a job description.

5. Compare your qualifications to the job's qualifications. Think about which of your accomplishments best align with what the prospective employer is looking for. Is this a realistic position for you?

### 11 Components Needed for a Powerful Cover Letter to Get Noticed

1. Contact information area

2. Date

3. Inside address (mailing address, with verified title and spelling)

4. Reference line

5. Salutation

6. Intro paragraph

7. Value-selling paragraph

8. Background summary with education and experience

9. Call to action statement/Closing paragraph

10. Appreciation statement/Complementary closing/Signature

11. Enclosures

You really have to "clinch the deal" within the first 15 seconds. Roughly speaking, that equates to the first paragraph. The trick is to try and differentiate yourself and your correspondence from all the other candidates vying for the position.

### Contact Information

1. Your contact information is where you supply the details about how a hiring authority can contact you. In today's high-tech world, you should include your physical address, phone number, cell phone number, and email address.

### Date

2. Date

### Inside Address

3. This is where you will put the prospective employer's mailing address. It is important that you verify everything—title, company spelling, address, whether they are an INC, LLC, corporation, etc. I personally feel that it is important to include all this information even if you are emailing your cover letter. Doing so raises the bar for you and sets a standard of professionalism that most job seekers are not taking the time out to do. It's just another way to differentiate yourself as a stronger candidate.

### Reference Line—RE: Job Title Applying For

4. This section is optional. My personal preference is to include it because it makes things clear and easy for the reader. You can use the popularly accepted abbreviation RE: (regarding/reference to). There is also the distinct possibility that if your reference line is well worded, it will bias the reader to spend more time looking at your paperwork. That's because you will have saved them some time by not forcing them to guess what job you're applying for. In the process, you appear clear, direct, and efficient to the reader.

### Salutation

5. Make sure you're using the correct salutation (Mr., Mrs., Ms.) for you contact. Whenever possible, try to have an actual contact person's name and title. Full names are preferred to avoid such impersonal salutations as "To Whom It May Concern."

### Intro Paragraph

6. Make sure your introduction paragraph:
    a. Is "interest generating," grasps the reader's attention, and compels them to continue reading
    b. States or implies the reasons you're interested in the specific position or organization to which you're applying

If you are able to use a referral's name in the first paragraph of your cover letter, know that it will substantially increase the reader's motivation to focus on your paperwork!

How do you best use a referral's name? The three easiest ways are to:

1) Use a personal contact's name (call to confirm) that you have obtained via . . .
    a) Industry association networking
    b) Professional association networking
    c) Literature research, PR articles, etc.
    d) Social Networking, Social Media

If you know the name of a personal contact you can mention in your introduction paragraph, then the odds are the hiring authority will read your letter with greater care. That's because they don't know what type of relationship you have with the person you mentioned, so they will "play it safe" and assume it's a close one.

2) Refer to some piece of knowledge you know about the organization that the average person would not know. (This information will come from your company research.)

Such a reference demonstrates a level of personal interest in the company that most employers do not see. As a result, it will differentiate you from the "crowd," and your letter will stand out.

3) Pay a **genuine** compliment.

Being complimentary will appeal to the hiring authority's sense of pride and will create interest in your cover letter. Try something like: "You strike me as someone who would be aware of the importance and value of a top National Account Manager." You are basically trying to "hook" the prospective employer's ego so that they read the rest of your letter. Compliments get your cover letter noticed.

### Value-Selling Paragraph

7. The value-selling paragraph:
   a. Demonstrates your ability to add value to the organization to which you are applying, relative to the company's needs as uncovered during your research
   b. Highlights your key strengths and abilities

This is where you must motivate the hiring authority to invite you in for an interview. List specific achievements and contributions that can transfer to a new job and that can be applied to the prospective employer's organizational needs.

In particular, share results you achieved in areas that are critical to good job performance in the organization you are contacting. In essence, you are providing proof that you have succeeded in these areas in the past and that you will bring value that will translate to another corporate environment.

For your value-selling paragraph to be most effective, you must understand the specific needs of the organization you're targeting. Use your networking contacts to help you uncover those needs.

Don't forget to research the answer to their needs for your top 12 companies (and their customer base and competitors). Some of the needs may be similar within the same industries, saving you time in having to reword this paragraph.

The value-selling paragraph is where you can briefly use your most relevant accomplishments to show a prospective employer how you can 1) Save them money, 2) Make them money, and/or 3) Solve a problem for them that is not currently being resolved.

The value-selling paragraph is the key area in which you will market yourself and demonstrate how you will bring value to the equation.

### Background Summary

8. The background summary is where you explain your relevant education and professional experience. You want the hiring authority reading it to understand that you possess the appropriate training, education, and experience to perform the tasks required of the position. Keep this section short, as your resume will cover all the same information in more detail.

### Call-to-Action Statement/Closing Paragraph

9. Here, toward the end of your cover letter, you must incorporate a statement that is a "call to action." In other words, you want to entice the employer to take favorable action in seriously considering you. You also want to indicate to them that you will be taking action and following up with them.

Once you are sure enough time has passed, call the prospective employer to determine if they are interested. If appropriate, arrange an interview. People always respect good follow-up, provided that you don't make yourself a nuisance.

My suggestion is to take the initiative in following-up. As I have mentioned before, your sense of urgency is usually different from the hiring authority's. This way, you are in the driver's seat, leaving nothing to chance. Being proactive also creates a great opportunity for you to gain a contact and start building a professional relationship with someone with whom you can network.

### Appreciation/Thank-You Statement

10. Before closing your cover letter, thank the reader for their time. Everyone is busy today and heartfelt appreciation is another way to set yourself apart. It shows that you are a courteous person who respects someone else's time.

After reading your cover letter, the prospective employer should have a very clear idea of why hiring you is a good decision!

### Enclosures

11. Mark the bottom of your cover letter, on the left, with the notation "Enclosures" if you are including your resume, a specific article of interest, or other documents that have been previously discussed and promised.

### How to Create Targeted Cover Letters

Targeting your cover letters to each job opportunity is ideally the best and strongest method. Here is where the in-depth research on the position and/or the company's culture and past hiring needs really pays off. You can now use that information to tailor your letter to each company.

The amount of research and thought you put into your cover letters will make the difference between getting an interview and having your paperwork ignored!

When you do your research, take the job listing and make a list of the skills and traits the employer is looking for. Then, examine your resume and look for a match with those same or similar skills and experiences. Tell the reader how your skills and qualifications match their job in either a paragraph or a bulleted list. I personally think bullets are faster and easier to read, but they can take up more space. Remember to keep your bullet points short. You need your cover letter to fit on one page if at all possible.

The main goal is to leave no doubt in the prospective employer's mind that you are qualified for the position. Feed them the information they need easily, clearly, and succinctly. Make it simple for them to see and read the information quickly. In other words, help make their job easy for them!

I suggest using italics, underlining, and bolding to help emphasize the most important points for the reader. Be careful not to overuse this idea. If you do, it will immediately diminish the technique and render your paperwork too distracting and "busy." (This same idea can be used sparingly on your resume.)

### Specific Guidelines for Writing Your Thank-You Letters

The thank-you letter is sent out following an interview. First, let me say that I know this is one of the areas most people tend to agonize over, the reason being a sense of pressure exists. That's because the stakes have risen. You're fully "in the game" now and you don't want to blow your chances.

Take the time you need to carefully word your thank-you note, but please remember to send it within 24 hours of your interview.

#### Who Should Receive a Thank-You Letter?

1. The hiring authority (prospective boss)

2. The interview team members

3. The staffing manager

4. Networking contacts

What are the benefits of a thank-you letter being sent to the hiring authority?
   a. It shows you have great follow-up skills.
   b. It shows you appreciate the time they spent with you.
   c. It's a great opportunity to market yourself and your relevant skills once again.
   d. It shows you are interested in and enthusiastic for the job!

The general format of your thank-you letter should follow these guidelines:

1. Express thanks and appreciation for the interview and the interviewer's time.

2. Reiterate interest in the position and employment with the company.

3. Reaffirm your relevant qualifications/experience.

4. Include a special value statement if possible.

5. Close with a final thank you.

What are the benefits of a thank-you letter to the interview team?

It's not as required as the previous letter, but this note of appreciation, again, will set you apart from the "crowd." It will also give you a definite competitive edge over the other candidates for the position. Another idea to give you a leg up on the competition is to follow up an emailed thank-you letter with a snail-mailed copy of the letter. Hand-address the envelope if your handwriting is legible. In that case, a hand-scripted thank-you note is a great touch. Whether typed or penned by hand, personalize these letters as much as possible, but keep them simple.

The general format of your thank-you letter should follow these guidelines:

1. Express thanks and appreciation for the interview and the interviewer's time.

2. Reiterate interest in the position and employment with the company.

3. Refer to a topic or event that occurred during the interview.

4. Show appreciation for information shared with you during the interview.

5. Close with a final thank you and reference of possibly working together.

When sending a thank-you letter to HR/staffing, the general format should follow these guidelines:

1. Express appreciation for arranging the interview.

2. State that you are interested in the position.

3. Include a brief value statement that emphasizes your ability to make a contribution to the organization.

4. Close with a final thank-you and state your interest in receiving a job offer.

What are the benefits of a thank-you letter to your networking contacts?

Here again, with some well-placed appreciation, you can really differentiate yourself from the pack. Most people network and get ideas/leads from others, but they rarely slow down long enough to go back and thank the person who helped them, let alone provide that individual with an update of how the lead worked out. It's just another way to get noticed and stand out from other job seekers.

When sending a thank-you letter to networking contacts, the general format should follow these guidelines:

1. Express appreciation for the help provided.

2. Offer feedback on the benefits your contact's help afforded you.

3. Update them on the status of your job search.

4. Request ongoing or additional help.

5. Close with a final thank-you statement.

### 15 Tips to Writing Cover Letters You Should Know

The traditional cover letter rules of thumb are as follows:

1. When contacting recruiters, HR reps, and cold networking contacts, use bullets for easier scanning.

2. When contacting HR managers, recruiters, and warm networking contacts (when you know the recipient will spend more time reading), use a paragraph letter style.

3. Use one-inch margins all around. (Some say ½- or ¾-inch.)

4. Keep paragraphs to five lines or fewer.

5. Consider changing the font size on bullet points so they're one to two sizes smaller than your text portion.

6. Suggested fonts (Use between 10–12 point.):
   Ariel*
   Garamond*
   Bookman Old Style
   Tahoma

Times New Roman
Verdana

7. Keep the interests of the reader in mind. The letter may be about you, but it's *for* them.

8. Communicate how you'll meet the recipient's needs or solve a problem rather than what you hope they will do for you.

9. Highlight your top three to five key points from your resume, using keywords and phrases. Don't repeat your resume but add information that is not on it.

10. Keep the use of "I" or "my" to a minimum. Try to use "you" or "your" so that you come across to your reader on more friendly terms.

11. Refer to the organization as "it" rather than "they."

12. Leave some breathing space in the letter for "visual relief."

13. Sign the original cover letter with blue ink and paperclip it to the resume.

14. Remember to follow up within three days of emailing or five days of mailing your cover letter. In your email subject line, include the position's title and your name. Include the cover letter within your email and as an attachment with your resume.

15. Remember that this is all good old-fashioned professional business etiquette!

### Additional Writing Advice

1. Write when you are fresh. Write during your prime time, whenever that is.

2. Write alone, without any distractions.

3. There are a lot of resources, particularly samples of cover letters, available online and in books. Turn to them for assistance.

4. As part of your Bonus Material for this chapter, you will find a list of related books I created for you that should be available at your local library. My suggestion is to browse through a few of them and then take the stronger books home to review. Create a folder titled "Cover Letter Samples/Examples" and include photocopies of the stronger examples to modify for your search needs.

5. Professional writers suggest writing your cover letter from the bottom up. That means you start with your closing paragraph, then include the real content of the letter, and finally finish up with the introductory paragraph.

   Try this approach and see if the letter-writing process becomes easier and faster for you.

6. Write a really great letter, recycle it when possible, and then tweak and customize it.

7. Rinse and repeat these techniques throughout your job search.

Again, the key is to differentiate yourself from the hordes of other job seekers. And one surefire way to accomplish that is with great follow-through and follow-up!

As you prepare to move on to the next chapter, try to get six to seven leads moving this week.

*Precision of communication is important,*
*more important than ever, in our era of hair-trigger*
*balances, when a false or misunderstood word may create*
*as much disaster as a sudden thoughtless act.*
—James Thurber

## Job Search Expert Action Plan

1 Take your reader Bonus Material for this chapter, "Powerful Letters That Get Noticed: Sweet Job Search Advice" book list to your local library. Check out 3–5 books that initially look the strongest relative to your needs. I am suggesting that number so that you will not be overwhelmed initially. This is an area that most job seekers find overwhelming and tedious.

2 At home, spend some time quietly picking ones that are your favorites to make photocopies of. Once you have made the copies, put them in your Job Search Expert Binder for Chapter 4, "Sample Letters."

3 Create a folder on your desktop marked "Job Search Cover Letters" or "JS Cover Letters."

4 Retype several of these letters from your binder into this computer folder. Modify the sample letters for your specific needs to have ready for your job search requirements as you go forward.

## Additional Job Search Notes

# CHAPTER 5

# Time Management:
# Tools and Tricks of the Trade

*Time is the scarcest resource and unless it is
managed nothing else can be managed.*

—PETER DRUCKER

LET'S OPEN THIS CHAPTER with a vocabulary lesson. What
is time management? Time management is the process of
managing what we are actually doing while time is ticking away.

Before we get started on any task, we set up expectations
of what we want to accomplish within a given period of time.
We make promises to and agreements with ourselves regarding
what we will accomplish within that timeframe. Then, when we
do not keep our promises, which we are so apt to do, we feel
like we have failed.

How do we prevent setting ourselves up for failure? First, we
need to ask ourselves if we're being realistic with the goals we
wanted to accomplish over the specified period of time.

I know that I personally tend to over-commit myself to goals
I cannot realistically complete in one day. Then, at times, I feel
like I have failed, when in fact, I really have not. For the most

part, I simply was not realistic about what I set out to accomplish in 24 hours.

Second, we need to ask, "Could I be better about how I'm using my time?" The answer to this question is where, I believe, the bulk of the solution lies.

Today I'm going to cover some good time management techniques that you can apply throughout the duration of your job search. Some of them you may already be doing, others you may not like, and still others you may try and love.

As we move forward in this chapter, I'm suggesting you keep an open mind. Commit to attempting the strategies I'm recommending for just 21 days. Why three weeks? It's a proven fact that for any true change to take place, you must practice the new habit that effects that change for 21 days before you can effectively adopt it.

Rome was not built in a day. Try to change only one habit at a time. Stay with it and maintain full focus on it. Wait the recommended 21 days to ensure that you have truly adopted the new habit and fully integrated it into your lifestyle.

In the next section of this chapter, I will discuss some time management tools that will help you with your job search. Some of those that I am about to describe will be easier for you to understand once you have downloaded your Bonus Material at the end of the chapter. That said; don't get hung up if you don't fully grasp some of them at first.

Even if some of these ideas don't first appeal to you, I am suggesting you try all of them. You can then modify them to work with your own individual style. Remember to give all these ideas a fair chance. Stick with them for at least a few days, ideally 21 days or more.

### Before You Start: Time-Saving Ideas

1. Clean off your desk. I did this yesterday. Cleaning off the top of your workstation helps clear the way for everything

that is to come. It actually frees you mind from the clutter so you can focus on more pressing matters.

Take the papers from the top of your desk and put them in a manila folder labeled with today's date (Month XX, 2011) TOP OF DESK. Make it a goal to go through that folder this upcoming Friday afternoon and take care of all its contents. What do I mean by take care of? I mean categorize all of the papers contained therein. Separate them into "Do It," "Delegate It," "Delay It," or "Dump It" piles. Try to handle the paperwork one time only. Make that one of your goals this week.

On each piece of paper in the folder, stick a POST-It note and write on it "Do It!", "Delegate" (need help to do), or "Delay It" (can wait). Those that are part of the "Dump It" pile can be thrown in the trash RIGHT NOW!

2. David Allen, the author of *Getting Things Done*, suggests a particular filing system. Brian Tracy and Jack Canfield use this same system. It goes like this . . .

To start off, you will need 43 manila folders. You will need to number each of them 1–31. This number corresponds to each day of the month. Next, mark the remaining 12 folders with the months of the year. What you're creating is a "perpetual" file into which you can offload all your documents, notes, reminders, and everything else job-related.

With the first set of folders, you're running a 31-day cycle from the current day. Anything extending beyond 31 days from today can then be filed into the appropriate month. So if today were October 6, you would be using folder #6 as your starting point.

Now suppose you have something happening six weeks from today. Then you would file that paper in the November folder. If, on the other hand, you need to call someone two weeks from today, you would put a note in the folder marked #20 for October 20th.

The process is similar to working with a day timer or calendar, except in this case, you can file working pieces of papers, notes, and documents into the appropriate folder. The overall system is a great idea, but it must be maintained on a daily basis.

So what happens at the end of every day? You move the items that are not yet completed in today's folder forward to the next day's folder. If you go out of town, you need to remember to move forward all the items that were left undone in your absence when you return.

The goal behind this idea is that you will not misplace your paperwork in the future. That's because you have a literal physical paper trail, which prevents your documents from getting misplaced. This paper management concept is one of the best ways to organize physical follow-up on your paperwork so that you will not lose it in the future. In a job search process, every day is a moving target when it comes to both events and paperwork. Every day, a new piece of information exists that needs to be tracked. This system keeps it all in order.

3. Another time-saving idea I suggest is to eliminate your metal file support and hanging Pendeflex® folders and use only manila folders. This eliminates the need to double file, hence saving you time. By using only manila folders, you no longer have to worry about labeling both the hanging folder and manila folder, thus labeling twice.

   This is an instance of do as I say not as I do. That's because I'm not sure if I can personally give up my hanging folders. Nevertheless, I'm intrigued with the idea. Is it a pain to have to label them and then keep resorting when you grow out of them? You bet! Ideally, if you are going to stay with your hanging folders, then put only one folder in each Pendeflex®.

Whatever system works for you is great. Just find one that's efficient for you. Studies show that as much as 30% of our time is spent looking for lost files or lost information. I believe that. A good filing system will free up that wasted time.

## Handling Email—How to Save Time

*Control your own time. Don't let it be done for you. If you are working off the in-box that is fed to you, you are probably working on the priority of others.*
—Donald Rumsfeld

In the process of moving my website www.Consumer CareerSearch.com to a new server, 23,000 of my emails got misplaced. As you can imagine then, this subject is very near and dear to my heart.

I usually like to get my emails down to about 3,000 at one time, but I currently have 12,000 in one of my accounts. That's actually not as bad as it sounds. It's very easy to find yourself reacting to emails that rob your time. We all really need to get into the habit of realizing that most emails can wait.

During the timeframe you have committed to working on your job search, remember to focus on your goals for that entire duration. If emails come through that are not related to your job search goals for that day, then do not address/reply to them until after dinnertime.

That's not to say that you should just let messages pile up in your inbox. Email is another form of incoming communication that needs to be processed and organized. You can approach this task the same way you did your physical paperwork—in terms of creating folders that will act as "processing stations."

When I focus on cleaning up my emails, I start by sorting them. I begin this process by clicking the "From" button. Organizing them this way makes it very easy to delete whole categories of message you know you don't need but have not made it to the "junk" and spam folder.

One new feature with Windows 7 and Norton is that Norton has begun pre-marking emails as spam to make it easier to filter and delete them. Be aware that this project can take some time until you're up to speed, so remember to do it *after* your normal workday hours or on the weekend.

To start, create folders over in your navigation bar where you want to file emails worth saving. When creating each new folder, make sure you are always at the top of the navigation bar. That way, folders will be alphabetized and will not inadvertently become a subfolder of something non-related.

Like all correspondence, when contending with email, deal with it only once. If you can take care of it in two minutes, do so. The experts say that you should be able to tackle one-third of your email this way.

Now create four more folders in your navigation bar: *ACTION*, *WAITING FOR*, *READ/REVIEW*, and *PRINT*.

Specific to your job search, you can also label four more files: *JSACTIVE *, *JSWORKING ON*, *JSWAITING ON*, and *JS ANSWERS*.

Note that when you use the asterisk before these folders' names, they will be alphabetized at the top of the folder list.

I suggest you BCC (blind carbon copy) yourself on all emails related to your job search. Either that or remember to forward them to yourself from your Send folder. When they reach your inbox, file them in the appropriate folder. You can also create a special folder for companies with which you have conducted a lot of activity.

Check all of these aforementioned folders I have suggested periodically to see if any of the items can be deleted. To make this whole process easier, make sure you're a good typist. If you are a slow typist, go to a community college and take a course. You want to be able to type at least 50 words a minute. This ability will save you a lot of time.

### How to Plan in Advance to Maximize Your Results

Start planning for tomorrow each afternoon. Every minute of preplanning you do today in preparation for tomorrow will save you five to 10 minutes in the execution of each activity you must complete tomorrow.

Let's take today for example. At 4:30 P.M., I want you to take out a legal pad. With a straightedge, draw a line down the paper one-third of the way into the pad from the left side. Your paper should now have two columns, divided one-third, two-thirds. On the top of the paper in the first column, write Phone. In the second, larger column, write Company Name/Contact Name. (You can create a separate column for the two if you prefer.) I have created a template to assist you here, "The Executive Job Search Experts Call List." You will find this material as one of your reader Bonus Materials.

My suggestion is to place your "A" company calls first and then follow them with you "B" list. You should try to list 40 people you are going to try to call tomorrow. The ones you do not get to tomorrow will get transferred to the next day's afternoon to-do list.

Again, you list the "A" contacts first followed by those on your "B" list. Collectively, this list will contain the people with whom you will spend the bulk of your morning trying to catch up, connect, and set up an initial interview. Because of its efficiency, this is the primary method major executive firms use.

Your "A" calls will be those where you are following up on an actual contact or lead. You have already spoken to this person, have been referred to them by someone, or must find out from them for a fact that an open position exists. These are your "hot" calls. They are you MUST calls.

Your "B" calls will consist of those individuals with whom, at this point, you do not have a relationship, or you lack valid information that any openings exist at their company. You do, however, have a contact name you need to validate. These are you SHOULD call.

Your "C" calls are the ones for which you Company/Contact Name column contains the least amount of information. In this case, you don't even have the name of a potential hiring authority. These are the calls that it would NICE to follow through on, but only if you have the time to do so.

Bear in mind that this is a classic case of the 80/20 rule. 20% of your daily activities will account for 80% of your job search results. For the best results, remember to focus on you top 20%.

A realistic goal here is to make five valid good, solid contacts with high-quality information per day. This aim, however, is easier said than done.

Studies have shown that fewer than 3% of all people have clear, concise goals, let alone have written them down. Further complicating matters, fewer than 1% ever re-evaluate or revise their goals. When you write down your daily job search goals, you program your subconscious to keep them in mind throughout the day.

> *Written goals transform you from a wandering*
> *generality into a meaningful specific.*
> —Zig Ziglar

With "The Executive Job Search Experts Call List" method, I am assuming you are currently either self-employed or unemployed and have the time to devote this level of time commitment to your job search. I would not necessarily recommend this method to an employed person, unless they were implementing it on Saturdays or Sundays while networking with friends.

At the end of the day, it's more important to finish some of your "A" calls than it is to complete all your calls at the price of not accomplishing any progress in your job search. Focus on completing one task. Then you can try to play a numbers game. **Quality leads and follow-up here are key.** In this particular instance, focus first on your "A"s before you move to your "B" and "C" lists.

At the end of each day, make a list of:

1. 5 things you accomplished today

2. 5 things you are grateful for

Once you have completed this list, find yourself a quiet, alone area 45 minutes before you go to bed at night to read it over. This will re-enforce positive energy from the day and will usher in the next day on a positive tone.

If you have the extra time and inclination, you can take your list a few steps further.

1. List five things you accomplished.

2. Come up with five things you're grateful for.

3. Review your goals.

4. Visualize the achievement of your job offer.

5. Define the five things you want to accomplish tomorrow.

Scientific research has shown that whatever you focus on in the last 45 minutes of the day has a large impact on both your sleep and your next day. The subconscious mind will process this late-night input up to six times more often than anything else you have experienced during the day.

When you drift off to sleep, you enter into what scientists call the alpha brain wave state of consciousness. At this time, your brain and subconscious memory are very suggestible.

That is why reading to children before they go to bed is so important. It helps them to wind down and fall asleep. In addition, most good children's books have lessons, messages, or morals that become a part of the child's conscience and sub-conscience while they're falling asleep.

Think about all the late-night cramming you did in school. I guess this tendency explains why it worked, at least for me.

### Daily Success Plan

You want to start at your desk no later than 8:00 A.M. if possible.

Start by reviewing your calendar, schedule, deadlines, and list of top five goals to complete today.

1. Begin with your most *urgent and important* calls or tasks.

2. Tackle those important calls or tasks.

3. Do your "Feared Thing First," or to quote Brian Tracy "Eat That Frog."

4. Remember to break down the overwhelming projects into smaller tasks and take each one a step at a time. Remember: "How do you eat an elephant? One bite at a time."

5. Maintain a sense of urgency.

6. Remember to check your list of five daily goals throughout the day to see how on track you are to completing them. Every time you finish one, cross it off your list. This will emphasize the accomplishment and will increase your positive internal energy level.

7. Keep track of all the new information you're gathering while getting in touch with the contacts on your list. Take notes during your phone calls. Enter the information you walk away with as soon as you get off the call by transferring it into your Excel spreadsheet. Alternatively, if you have a good memory, you can allot time at the end of the day for this task.

8. Take small breaks. Try not to have lunch at your desk.

9. Remember to keep all papers you are not working on off your desk.

10. At 4:30 P.M., remember to start preparing your list of calls and follow-up activities for the next day using "The Executive Job Search Experts Call List" sheet.

11. Document five things you accomplished today.

12. Document what follow-up occurred today or needs to occur as a result of the calls and projects you completed.

13. Handle your follow-through and correspondence to follow up from what transpired during the day.

As a recruiter, I traditionally make my "cold calls" in the morning and my follow-up calls in the afternoon. Why? People tend to be more responsive in the mornings than the afternoons. Make your important calls take place the morning before people become too distracted or tired.

**RECRUITER TIP:** If you're trying to get a hold of people on the phone, the following time slots are good guidelines to try and catch most people:

**7:45–8:15** A.M.
8:15–8:55 A.M.
11:30 A.M.–12:05 P.M.
1:00–1:35 P.M.
**4:30–6:00** P.M.

When sending emails, time them to arrive around:

**7:30** A.M. **Tuesday–Friday**
10:30 A.M.–1:15 P.M.
4:30–6:00 P.M.

At the end of each week, try to get into the habit of reviewing the week's activity. I suggest you try to do this mid-afternoon on Friday. I would set up an appointment for yourself in 28 days at around 4:30–5:30 P.M. to review and analyze your job search results for the "month." Ideally, it's easier if you do this with a calendar month, at the true last day of the month.

## Weekly Success Plan

Ideas for your list:

1. Clean desk and loose papers.

2. Complete all filing and move everything forward in the 43 manila folders if you are using this method.

3. Download or transfer any ideas from the week that you have not already entered into your job search idea book. This is a spiral book, measuring approximately 5 x 7.5 inches, where any ideas worth looking into that come to mind relative to your job search are captured during the week. You want to confirm that these ideas are being acted on and researched further.

4. Evaluate your big action plans. Decide which are complete and which are incomplete.

5. Make sure you have moved forward, updated your calendar, and marked all action items from calls made during the week.

6. Review your "Waiting For" list.

7. Review your list of New Contacts/Companies ideas.

8. Make a list of anything that happened this past week that you could have done better.

9. Give yourself some type of small treat and acknowledge what you did accomplish this past week.

Scoring an actual interview deserves an extra-special something.

10. Remember to cut yourself some slack.

A job search can be a grueling, tedious process but do not give up. Looking for a job is an extremely unstructured process. Everyone kind of makes it up as they go along. As I have mentioned, your job search is an ongoing work in progress, one that you must fine-tune on a daily basis.

Progress will happen much faster if you create some disciplined systems to help you keep on track. You need to stay with the task and track any information associated with it. You do not want to let any of the clues get away. The ability to accurately prioritize and follow through is another key issue. That is why I'm suggesting the systems and tools I have discussed in this chapter.

One name with a phone number on a scrap of paper could be the lead you are looking for. Don't let that opportunity slip away. You need to create a good, solid system to keep track of all the information you are uncovering. Then you have to remember to follow up and follow through. That is the key.

Persistence and follow-through will pay off in the end. Do not give up.

Before closing this chapter, I would like to leave you with a quote:

*The secret to success is to do the common things uncommonly well.*
—John D. Rockefeller, Jr.

That assertion holds true when YOU efficiently and effectively manage your time as much as possible as opposed to allowing every moment of your day to be a reaction to an action.

A plan to achieve your daily goals will get you closer to the big aim of landing that next great job!

## Job Search Expert Action Plan

1   Start by printing 10 copies of "The Executive Job Search Experts Call List™" to work with on your desk. Keep these in the front inside pocket of your binder or in a folder labeled "JSE Call List."

2   On a daily basis, date the list(s) you are working on that day.

3   At the end of the day, put the old sheet back into your Job Search Expert Binder in one of the extra tab areas. Mark that tab "JSE Call Lists."

CHAPTER **6**

# Internet Tools to Turbo Charge Your Job Search

## Effective Job Search Internet Techniques

*People are always blaming their circumstances for what they are. I don't believe in circumstances. The people who get on in this world are the people who get up and look for the circumstances they want and if they can't find them—make them!*

—GEORGE BERNARD SHAW

THE INTERNET IS THE SINGLE LARGEST research resource for the job seeker. That is the good news; the bad news is that, at times, the amount of information can be overwhelming and distracting.

From personal experience, I know I can easily find myself going down one path and then ending up at another that is somewhat related but not really the exact information I was looking for.

When utilizing the internet to assist you on your job search, remember to stay focused. If you find yourself suddenly on a website that is only somewhat relevant to your original question, bookmark it in your browser's favorites or make a note to come back to it later. Then get back on track!

In the earlier days of the internet, initially everyone tended to believe whatever information they read there. By and large, people now realize that not everything "published" on the internet is accurate.

When doing research for your job search—or any research for that matter—on the internet, remember to weigh the caliber of the information. To do so, ask yourself these questions:

1. How recent is the information?

   When you're dealing with the business of information, much of it is already old by the time you get it. With traditional printed publications your information is usually 12–18 months old. It takes a year to publish most business research books. The internet is better in this area, due to the fact that you will find more current information available on the internet. Try to stay with information that is less than six months old.

   With this recession, I have professionally seen more outdated information relative to job search statistics. The metrics involving the job search have changed during this recession, and most the internet information has not caught up with the process's current statistics.

2. Does the "author" of the information have a valid professional background relative to the topic?

3. Are there valid sources listed by the writer? Can the information be verified?

4. Does the information found on the site relate to any site advertising? Is the information artificially slanted to support the bias of the advertiser?

5. Does the site look professional and grammatically accurate?

See source: www.library.jhu.edu/

## Gateways and Portals You Need to Be Aware Of

When you're beginning your job search research, I suggest you visit some of the main gateways, or what I call "portals," for your job search information.

This is by far the fastest way to find good general information for your job search needs. Remember to stay focused and on task regarding the informational answers you are seeking. Here are some of my go-to career-hunting sites:

1. www.job-hunt.org (large but overwhelming)

2. www.jobhuntersbible.com (Mark and Richard Bolles)

3. www.rileyguide.com (Margaret Riley Dikel)

4. www.careeronestop.org (U.S. Department of Labor)

5. www.careerjournal.com (*Wall Street Journal* executive website)

6. www.quintcareers.com (lightly touches upon a lot of topics)

7. www.jobstar.org (California based and oriented)

8. www.cacareerzone.org (California oriented—provides a choice of viewing the site via text, graphic, or Flash mode)

## Directories You Should Be Using

Another important piece in the internet research resource puzzle is directories. The nice thing about directories is that the information contained in them is sorted by humans and not "spiders." As a result, they will give you a fair amount of good, broad information. Again, however, you will need to do some comparison shopping. Check a couple of them out and decide which ones work best for your particular job search needs. My three favorite directories are:

1. www.dmoz.org (This is supposed to be one of the largest.)

2. www.lii.org (librarians internet index—used to be www
   .ipl2.org)

3. www.infomine.ucr.edu/ (University of California Riverside)

### Where to Go for More In-Depth Information

The following websites will help you gather more information
about those top 25–50 companies you're targeting on your "hot"
wish list (i.e., the companies you would really like to work for):

1. www.CareerOneStop.com (U.S. Government website)

2. www.CEOExpress.com

3. www.Weddles.com/associations/index.htm (associations)

4. www.Ipl.org (On home page in search box enter "industry
   associations" to get to list of industry associations.)

5. www.bls.gov/oco/cg/home.htm (provides available careers
   by industry, etc.)

6. www.hoovers.com (provides the competitors for each
   company you check out)

7. www.edgaronline.com

8. www.asaenet.org (American Society of Association
   Executives—shows more than 300 industries)

In addition, don't forget to use www.Goggle.com. In particular, take advantage of their "Advance Search" tool.

### Company Internet Research

During the process of your job search, you will need to gather
more information on companies that:

1. You are interested in working for

2. You have applied for jobs with

3. You are going to interview with

4. Are competitors of the firms you are talking to so you can better understand the product category and industry

I suggest the following websites to help you with your research:

1. www.kompass.com (2.4 million companies worldwide listed)

2. www.vault.com (job website with company info)

3. www.thomasnet.com

### The True Art of Uncovering People Using the Internet

#### Finding People You Know

In the course of your employment search, you will want to find people you have known over the years to network with. Over time, you may have lost touch with some of these individuals. In that case, it may require a bit of digging to locate them.

And yet, the effort is well worth it. That's because networking is one of the most effective ways to land your next job.

The following websites should prove helpful in assisting you in finding your lost contacts:

1. www.yellow.com (particularly versatile in terms of the different ways you can approach your search)

2. www.zoominfo.com

#### Finding People You Do Not Yet Know

If you're trying to find the name of an individual in a particular company whom you do not yet know, here are some suggestions on how to locate them:

1. Visit chat rooms.

2. Scout out forums and message boards.

3. Join newsgroups.

4. Hang out at networking websites, especially Social Media ones.

5. Leverage mailing lists.

## Job Search Engines

Some specific job search engines use spiders on the internet. They exist solely to build an index of jobs that are posted on multiple sites by compiling them into one convenient location. Make sure you do not apply to the same job through more than one site. Track your responses in your Excel sheet to avoid duplications.

You should look into:

- www.indeed.com
- www.simplyhired.com
- www.jobmaps.us
- www.jobster.com
- www.careerjet.com
- www.airsdirectory.com

### 7 Steps for Job Search Internet Success

1. If at all possible, create an email account that uses a professional-sounding name and is not tied into your work environment. I suggest using your first name and last name, such as eleanorsweet@email.com or eleanor .sweet@email.com.

2. If there are specific directions regarding the mechanics on how to apply to the jobs you're interested in, follow them exactly per their request. This is not the time to be a rebel and appear difficult. The hiring authority will not be interested in you as a candidate if you do not seem as though you have the ability to follow simple instructions.

   If the job description does not specify whether to send your resume as an attachment or in the body of the email, then you should do both. If the employer asks for your resume to be placed in the body of your email, then do a "cut and paste" and put your resume in the body of the message. At the end of your message, you can always tell them that you have a professional, fully formatted hardcopy version available upon request.

If the hiring authority is asking for a PDF file and you need a free converter, go to www.cutepdfwriter.com and download the software.

To convert your document, you will go to "print" and save it from your printer menu under "Cutepdfwriter." When you highlight and hit enter, the document is then converted into a PDF file.

3. When you save your resume, save it on your hard drive with your first and last name as part of the document name (e.g., PattySmithResume.doc or SmithPattyResume .pdf). Such a naming convention will make it easier for the person receiving it to keep track of it and find it later.

4. In the subject line of the email, be short and specific to make things easier for the hiring authority (e.g., Product Manager: Rick Stevens).

5. If possible, create an email signature that includes your contact information such as name, email address, and phone number.

To create a signature file in Microsoft Outlook, go to Tools, Options, and then Mail Formats. The information you place there will then automatically be put into the body of all your emails.

6. Double check that you are sending your resume to the correct person. Perform a spell check and make sure your computer "address book" did not inadvertently pick another person whose name is close in the alphabet.

7. Make sure you're not using a spam blocker, thereby creating problems for the person to whom you are sending your resume.

## 13 Steps: Daily Internet Success System

1. Apply for jobs on the internet 24–36 hours after they've initially been posted. The rationale here is that most people apply on the first day. If you do the same thing, you'll get lost in the sea of resumes the hiring manager is being overwhelmed with.

2. Check your email first thing in the morning, mid-afternoon, and at the end of the day, around 5:30–6:00 P.M. Lots of times, the hiring managers are tied up in meetings all day and do not have time to reach out and contact people until they are out of their meetings.

3. Respond immediately to any emails from hiring managers and recruiters.

4. Check your voicemail several times during the day and when you are on break from work.

5. Also check your physical mailbox for letters or postcards asking you for an interview or requesting you to fill out the enclosed job applications.

6. Update your Excel spreadsheet with new information regarding resumes sent/posted or people who have called you back.

7. When companies ask you to apply directly on their website, it is because they want you to complete an online application instead of submitting a resume. They are using a software program that keeps track of the hiring process from the time you apply until you receive a job offer. In this case, just do a "cut-and-paste process" from your saved resume or cover letter.

8. Plan to follow up seven to 14 days after you have applied via email. In the follow-up email, you want to reaffirm your interest in the position and receive confirmation that they did, in fact, receive your resume or application. Do not, however, bombard them with a lot of messages.

9. If you are able to figure out a contact name and phone number, call the hiring authority first thing in the morning before they get into a lot of meetings, preferably between 8:00 and 9:45 A.M. Make this call seven to 14 days after you have sent your cover letter and resume.

10. If you know someone within the organization, you can ask them to help you follow up on the status of your resume.

11. If you are in a major public database, you can repost your resume online, every seven to 10 days. Doing so will make it look like you've just recently entered the job market.

12. Set up automatic job alerts on the websites where you are registered. This strategy will help free up some of your time.

13. Keep checking the website of your "hot/wish list" companies to see if any new job listings related to your area of expertise have been posted.

Following are some additional internet tools and techniques to consider:

- Consider using a service like www.mozy.com ($5.99/month) to back up your computer and to gain remote access to your files if you happen to be out of town interviewing. Also try www.gotomypc.com ($9.95/month).
- Look into Google Documents (free). If you have Microsoft Office, you should be able to use Microsoft Live Workspace (free).

- Create a folder (e.g., in your email program) such as: Resume sent (You can either move from send or BCC yourself and then move from your inbox into this folder.)

### Internet Resume Tips

Be prepared to invest in a professional-looking interview-version resume that is formatted and printed on quality paper. You should also have an alternate version that is formatted for email submission.

Basically there are three current types of resume formats:

1. Traditional resume—This is the one you will leave at the end of your interviews. It contains action verbs and accomplishments customized to the particular job for which you are applying, based on all the research you have conducted on the organization, business culture, management, position, etc.

2. Scan able or text resume—This one is a simpler version of your traditional resume. It is saved in plain text to make it easier to be scanned into a database. Here, you will focus on key nouns, phrases, and accomplishments.

3. Web-based resume—This one is hosted on a domain (e.g., Monster.com) where anyone will have remote access to it at any time. You can publish this type of resume on your own website in addition to places such as:
   - www.geocities.com
   - www.freewebspace.net—This is a search engine that will show you other free web space hosting.

### How to Create a Scannable or Text Resume

1. Pick one of the following font types in size 11–14 point: Courier, Times, Helvetica, Futura, Arial, Optima, Palatino, or Univers. The idea is to pick a clean, easy-to-read type style for both the reader and the scanner.

2. Try to limit the number of characters per line to 65, if possible. This stipulation will be affected by the type and size of font you choose.

3. Left justify your text.

4. Eliminate any shading or graphics that are in your traditional resume.

5. Keep the format simple. The less complicated the better.

6. Capitalize all your major headings.

7. Do not bold, underline, or italicize.

8. Bullets should not be used in this version.

9. For a two-page resume, make sure to place your name at the top of each page. If your pages get separated for some reason during the scanning process, you'll increase the likelihood that they'll be reunited. Number your pages 1 of 2 and 2 of 2.

10. Make sure your resume is printed using a laser or inkjet printer. Do not use a dot-matrix printer.

11. Use 8½ x 11 white paper. The white background will give you the best contrast with the ink. A very pale-colored paper can be used as a backup.

12. Always send original copies and sign your cover letter in blue ink.

13. If at all possible, mail or hand-deliver your resume in a flat envelope. Do not staple multiple pages; use a standard-size paperclip.

### How to Format a Scannable/Text Resume

Remember that there will be no formatting with your scan-able resume. That is done only with your traditional resume.

You will be including all the sections you used in your traditional resume, such as name, address, contact information, summary qualifications, work experience, education, and additional professional training or specialized expertise or certifications (computer skills, etc.).

1. Use common industry terms and acronyms (jargon). Doing so helps highlight your experience and skills.

2. Include job-specific keywords that are important to the position or industry, bearing in mind that they will likely be used by the employers to specifically find candidates for that position.

3. Again, think of adjectives and nouns that the employer might use such as results-oriented, professional-selling, account manager, strategic planning, business development, marketing research, etc. Phrases such as under budget, successfully developed, and surpassed goals are also good ones.

4. It's a good idea to list a "Summary of Accomplishments" or "Key Skills" section. This is just another opportunity to leverage nouns, phrases, and industry terminology (jargon) that might be searched by the prospective employer.

5. When using abbreviations, be sure to also spell them out to cover both scan-able and readable versions of your resume.

Most companies will give you specific guidelines they want you to follow when submitting a text-based resume on their website.

The email version should be Courier font, single-spaced, 12 pt., with 65 characters to a line. For more information on the specifics of setting up your internet resume, see www.job-hunt .org/internetresume.html.

Most resume that are submitted today on the major websites are first "read" by a computer before a human reads them. This computerized scan weeds out non-contenders by seeing if the keywords in the resume match the keywords in the job posting.

My suggestion is that you consider adding the subhead "Keywords" followed by a series of keywords at the bottom of your resume type. Separate these keywords by commas. You should limit this section to two lines, using two- to three-word phrases in addition to single keywords. This concept is similar to that employed when writing a blog for the search engines, where you list "tags" and "categories" when you post a blog.

By being selective with your keywords, you will not compromise the quality of your resume's readability by artificially "stuffing" it with keywords. For customization purposes, you can also quickly change the keyword section to reflect the specific job position you're responding to.

### Inside Scoop: What Most Job Seekers Don't Know!

Eighty-nine percent of all job seekers apply to both Monster.com and CareerBuilder.com.

Only 4–10% of those individuals who apply to internet job postings get hired (and the higher 10% is for those in IT). In the past, a lot of people made the mistake of thinking the internet was the solution to their job search when actually it is just another job search avenue. When interviewed prior to the recession, hiring managers said that less than one out 1,000 hires came from the job boards. You can imagine that during this past recession those numbers increased to about 1,300–1,500.

The jobsites are not always what they appear to be:

1. Not all the jobs are real.

2. Some job postings are merely for brand image, meaning the companies posting want their competitors to think they're hiring, when in fact they really are not.

3. The jobs that are posted are often the more challenging ones, the less desirable ones, or those that require a higher level of experience and education.

Try not to spend more than 5% of your job search time with Monster and CareerBuilder.

There are those who say you should not spend more than 2.5% of your time on the internet. I would say to just make sure the time you do spend online is truly productive and not distracting you into areas that are draining your attention away from other avenues that will provide more tangible results.

Sometimes the internet can become an avoidance technique. It can give you a sense of false accomplishment, thereby deterring you from harder tasks that should be addressed and tackled.

Be honest with yourself and step away from the computer.

I am not sure there is a hard and true number of how much time you should ideally spend online. It constantly amazes me how much of our daily communication relies on email, internet research, social networking sites, etc.

Use your judgment. When in doubt, track your time and results for a two-week period and see what they tell you. See if you are getting valid tangible results from your time on the internet. Remember that like everything, the time you spend on the internet is a snapshot in time.

To quote, Richard N. Bolles, author of *What Color is Your Parachute?* "Job-hunting is not a science; it is an art." Naturally, some will be better at it than others.

"Job hunting is always a mystery." You will never totally understand why sometimes things will work and other times the same methods will seem fruitless.

"Job hunting often depends on some amount of pure blind luck!"—Richard N. Bolles. I agree.

Shift your focus to other approaches, such as networking. Experts suggest that in this current new economy, over 60–70% of jobs are landed through some form of networking.

Most people know 150–250 people. Those individuals are the start of your sphere of influence. Think of the possibilities. Do the math.

*Our achievements of today are but the sum*
*total of our thoughts of yesterday. You are today where*
*the thoughts of yesterday have brought you, and you will*
*be tomorrow where the thoughts of today take you.*
—Blaise Pascal

## Job Search Expert Action Plan

1 Go to your reader Bonus Material for this chapter, "Job Search Internet Sites You Should be Using." Spend the next six days you plan to work on your job search familiarizing yourself with one of the six websites sections listed in this document. Allow yourself no more than an hour to explore the sites for each section that day. Start Day 1 with "Gateways/Portals."

2 This is a job search project where you want to be careful not to get lost and waste time on areas that are not really going to help your current search needs.

3 Print off copies of information you think will assist your job search from the sites you visit.

4 File these printed documents, by subject matter, into the corresponding tabbed areas of your Job Search Expert Binder.

## Additional Job Search Notes

# PART 3

# Job Search
# Success Strategies

# CHAPTER 7

# Target Companies: How to Find, Manage, Research, and Succeed!

*The intelligent man is always open to new ideas. In fact, he looks for them.*
—PROVERBS 18:15

DURING YOUR JOB SEARCH, if you want to arm yourself with good, quality information, you will need to do extensive research on your target companies. This information will then guide your decisions throughout your entire job search process.

### Target Company Research Success Strategy

1. Your initial research should be broad.

   You will need to start with a wide research area to gather enough ideas into your "net." You do not want to make the initial decision, right out of the gate, of being too narrow with the companies you are considering. This tendency will slow down your search process. In the beginning, more is better in terms of potential company ideas and industries you are going to consider contacting. At the outset of your search, you need a large pipeline. On your initial list, set a goal of approximately 100 to 200 ideas for companies to target.

2. Update your target company list constantly.

As you continue to gather more information in your research, you will be able to divide your potential companies and industries into "A," "B," "Maybe," and "Discard" lists. The more research you do, the better your decisions and choices will be. I suggest you create these lists in an Excel spreadsheet or a Word Document. You will need to constantly update your lists as you continue to update your data on the organizations and executives. This task will be part of your *ongoing* research. At this point, once you have narrowed and refined your "A," "B," and "Maybe" lists, you should have approximately 75 to 100 companies. Use the Excel spreadsheet you downloaded from your Bonus Material *to assist you*

3. Never stop updating your lists or researching the companies you are actively interested in hearing about and interviewing with.

Research that is constantly updated and that is as current as possible will give you a competitive edge. You never want to stop updating your research. Keep researching right up until you return your signed offer letter. Knowledge is power! That's never more so than in this case. The more well-versed you are about an organization, its customers, its competitors, and its marketplace, the stronger you will come off during the interviewing process. Being well-informed shows you care, that you are motivated to do the homework, that you are a top-class professional, and that you're knowledgeable about the firm and its business.

Today I am going to focus more on target companies as opposed to target jobs. Some of the same principles will apply to both. I'm assuming at this point that most of you already know what types of positions you realistically qualify for. Then there are those of you who have finished your career-change assessments and are now realistic about what job titles you should be considering in this latest career move.

We will discuss target job research and career changes in another book. In the meantime, for those of you who are considering a major career change or are looking to stretch your background to better suit the marketplace, I would suggest you visit America's Career InfoNet online (www.acint.org/acinet). Use their Skills Profiler (for career changers and new grads) and/or Industry Information (for those who know which industry they want to research) sections.

To help you visualize target companies, I would like you to draw a circle with two outer circles around it on a sheet of paper. Label the center circle "A," the next circle "B," and the third circle "C."

### How to Create and Manage Your Target Company Contacts

A target company or organization is one to which your recent and past professional skills will easily transfer. These are companies and organizations where you "can hit the ground running" with your professional background.

### Target Companies "A"

Your "A" companies would be those that:

- Are in similar industries
- Make similar products
- Have similar customer bases
- Use similar manufacturing processes
- Employ similar channels of distribution
- Adopt similar operating styles

- Have similar corporate cultures
- Have similar corporate sales sizes and/or number of employees
- Are competitors

This group would be your "A" circle, the bull's-eye. It will contain your "A" target companies list.

First, I would like you to research your current and past employers' Standard Industrial Classification (SIC) codes. You can conduct this research at the library with their resources. In addition, you can do it online through the U.S. Department of Labor website (www.osha.gov/pls/imis/sicsearch.html).

In addition, you can also try the following websites:

- www.ReferenceUSA.com
- www.LexisNexis.com

Second, look up all your past and present professional competitors' SIC codes. Third, look into your target companies' customers and vendors as additional good targets.

Combine your first and second group of SIC codes into one list. Now look up all the companies in your geographical area with those SIC codes.

This is your list of "A" target companies, which will go in your circular bull's-eye. Hopefully you will have 25 to 50 names for your core list.

### Target Companies "B"

For your "B" list of companies, you want to think of companies that:

- Are in related industries (e.g., professional landscaping versus lawn and garden)
- Produce related product lines (e.g., pharmaceutical versus OTC (over the counter))

- Have related customer bases (e.g., drug stores versus mass merchants)
- Use related manufacturing processes
- Employ related channels of distribution [e.g., food (grocery) versus alcohol (sold in grocery and liquor stores)]
- Have varying corporate sales sizes and/or number of employees and in some way are related to the type of companies you have professional experience with (e.g., smaller or larger in company sales and employees than current or previous employers)

By the time you are done, you should have about 50 to 75 firms on this list.

### Target Companies "C"—"Maybe" Firms

Your "C" list will be companies that you have picked primarily for their geographic location. They are a long shot in terms of synergism with your professional history, industry experience, and product background.

This list will consist of companies that are primarily in your geographic area, that are in high-growth industries, or that you may have a personal contact in. It will most likely have 25 to 50 potential companies listed on it.

Since these firms are most likely long shots, I suggest you research them last, with the exception of the ones where you have a personal contact. In that case, contact the person you know after you have researched their organization in depth/detail.

As your job search progresses, you will find yourself constantly shifting companies from one list to the other and/or eliminating them to a discard list. Keep that discard list on the off chance that you received inaccurate information about the organization or something major changes there, suddenly causing the organization to become a viable target company again.

Once your search has been underway for about a month, you should find that you have about three to five good, valid leads at one time. These leads will consist of actual jobs, actual referrals, actual contacts, or a somewhat validated rumor of a position being added in the near future (30 days or less).

Based on your initial research, you will now find that you have about 25 to 35 companies in your "A" list that are very strong fits relative to your past professional experience. Meanwhile, your broader list of "B" target companies should still be about 50 to 100 additional firms, and you should be constantly adding to it.

## 9 Tools for Your Target Company Research

### Library Field Trip

Next, let's go over some of the various research sources that are available at most local libraries.

Get to know the best research librarian(s) in your local library. Interview them personally. Tell them about your job search. Then ask them to show you the best research tools they have, both in the library and online through their library website.

You need to understand that in most cases, by physically going to the library, you will have much better and broader access to most of these database-oriented websites than you would by remotely accessing the library's website from home. That's because the majority of companies have created limited remote access to their databases for library patrons.

Some of the resource tools you should find at most libraries, both public and private, are:

1. Business directories—You will find that some of these are free while others are fee-based. Your library may have a subscription that your library card allows you access to. In some cases, you can log in to your library's website remotely and gain access to some of these tools that way. With some of the fee-based directories, however, you will have to be physically present at the library to access

them. There again, your librarian can explain all of these specifics to you.

### Financial and Business Directories
- www.CareerSearch.com
- www.Edgar-online.com (SEC filings)
- www.Hoovers.com
- www.standardandpoors.com/home/en/us
- www.valueline.com

### Manufacturing and Service Directories
- Billion Dollar Directory
- Corporate 1000
- Directory of Corporate Affiliations
- International Directory of Corporate Affiliations
- Million Dollar Directory (three volumes)
- Moody's Index
- Directory of Manufacturers and Services by state
- Dun's Directory of Service Companies
- Directory of Consultants and Consulting Organizations
- Directory of Executive Recruiters

### Technical Directories
- Directory of American Research and Technology

### Research Public and Private Companies
- Corporate Information—www.corporateinformation .com/home.asp (free but requires registration)
- Dun & Bradstreet—www.dnb.com/us/
- Securities and Exchange Company and People Search— www.sec.gov/edgar/searchedgar/companysearch.html
- Million Dollar Database—www.dnbmdd.com/mddi/
- 123 Jump—www.123jump.com (global market news)
- Financial Web—www.financialweb.com

- GrayMetalBox—www.graymetalbox.com/s1/servlet/ com.scs.gray.StockLink?symbol=att
- Thomas Register—www.Thomasnet.com
- Hoovers—www.hoovers.com
- Forbes 500—www.forbes.com
- Business Week—www.businessweek.com
- Lexis Nexis—www.lexisnexis.com
- The Red Book—www.redbooks.com/Nonsub/Brand Search.aspx

### Venture Capital Directories
- Pratt's Guide to Venture Capital Sources (library suggestion)
- Venture's Guide to International Venture Capital

### Startup Venture Groups (to uncover which startup industries are getting funding)
- The MoneyTree Report—www.pwcmoneytree.com/ MTPublic/ns/index.asp
- PE Week Wire—www.privateequityweek.com
- Just Sell—www.justsell.com

2. Newspapers and magazines—You should look at the *Wall Street Journal, the New York Times, Fortune, Forbes, Crain's Chicago/Cleveland Business, Federal Career Opportunities, Federal Jobs Digest,* and Inc. to start with. Look up their various websites for online access.

    Check out:
- www.newslink.org
- www.cnbc.com
- www.money.com
- www.finance.yahoo.com
- www.marketwatch.com
- www.foxbusiness.com

3. Trade Journals—There are specialized trade journals for most industries. *Information Week, HomeWorldBusiness,*

*HFN, Hardware Retailing Magazine, Home Channel News,* and *Real Estate Professional* are several examples. If they do not have the trade journal you are interested in at the library, search for it online.

In addition, look up industry trade journals, for example, www.specialissues.com/lol/.

4. Local business journals and publications—One of the main national ones to check out is www.bizjournals.com.

5. Major newspapers are another source that most people forget about in today's world. Don't forget that newspapers and magazines often have special issues that can provide a wealth of information. Within their pages, you can "mine" out great information. Examples would be "Top 100 Retailers," "Fastest Growing Companies in Houston," etc.

6. Books about careers—Most of today's libraries have a special section set up where the entire job search/career books have been shelved in one location. If that's not the case at your library, your librarian can tell you where they are located on the shelves.

7. Market Resource Firms through your library will be another best bet.
   - www.aberdeen.com
   - www.business.com
   - www.Forrester.com
   - www.gartnergroup.com
   - www.idg.com

8. "Phone books"—Yellow Pages
   - www.Superpages.com (merged with Big Book)

9. Internet Libraries
   - Internet Public Library—www.ipl.org
   - The Digital Librarian—www.digital-librarian.com/

## Target Company Contacts

While you are researching your target companies, you also need to be researching the name of a contact person. You must also make sure this individual is a decision maker. The contact person you target should be at least two levels above your position.

You can never go wrong with the president, although realistically it can at times be tough to catch up with them, more so in the larger organizations. My suggestion is to avoid human resources as much as possible. In the larger organizations, try for an executive vice president instead.

Remember that no matter how your contact is uncovered, you must call the company to confirm that that person is still there and that you have the correct spelling of his or her name and the right title, address, and phone number. If you are unable to confirm this information through the receptionist, then ask to speak to the assistant of the person you are trying to contact. This next person, the assistant, will usually prove more helpful.

Figure that any information you uncover online or in a book will be at least a year old. As such, it is very important that you call each company directly prior to mailing or emailing anything out. The majority of the time, you should get through to an actual employee to confirm your designated contact person's name, title, and mailing address.

While you have this individual on the line, try to get the email address of your contact as well, if you have not been able to uncover it yourself. I will be upfront with you and tell you that most companies are unwilling to share email addresses, but it is worth a try. Alternatively, you can make an educated guess. If you uncover one person's email address within the organization simply mimic it. It's a long shot but worth the try if you're set on going the email route.

Now all that remains is getting the names you have not been able to uncover during your company research and your phone calls.

## Tools for Uncovering Contact Names

1. You will most likely uncover some contact names through the resources I have mentioned earlier in this chapter.

2. Don't forget to go to each company's website. It always amazes me how much information is available on corporate websites with respect to their executives.

3. Use Social Media to research executives at your target companies. If you do not know the person, then see if one of your connections knows someone within the company.

    I still have a strong professional bias toward LinkedIn over Facebook and Twitter. I do not, however, think Facebook and Twitter should be ignored if you are a "free agent." You never know where your next interview will come from.

4. Use the Google or Alexa search tools.
    a. At Google.com, go into the Advanced Search (www.google.com.au/advanced_search).
    b. In the top box, enter the company name.
    c. In the third box, type the title two levels above your title (your boss's boss's title).
    d. Go back to Google's Advanced Search and put the first and last names of the person you've uncovered on the first line.
    e. Put the company's name on the third line.
    f. Run the search.
    g. This strategy will give you some background information on your target contact.

These are some starter ideas on how to approach your target companies and organizations. If you are currently frustrated with the results so far in your job search, then now may be the time to start with a fresh slate.

You may have been doing all of this when you first started your search, but perhaps you have fallen off the wagon and gotten less disciplined over time. I know that one of the secret keys to a successful job search is a combination of a strong sense of discipline and persistence.

Take a second look at your search. Re-evaluate your target companies. Maybe there are some ways you could and should expand your list by widening your net.

### 7 Step Process to Contacting Your Target Companies

1. Mail 40 letters or fewer at a time. This approach will make your follow-up more manageable. Try emailing first, next phone, then mail, and finally follow up again with phoning.

2. Remember that you are only going to be sending your paperwork to someone who is two levels or more above you on the corporate ladder. Try to avoid sending your credentials to human resources.

   If you're dealing with a small company or if you are a senior executive, mail your resume directly to the president. You can never go wrong with this approach. Your resume gets noticed more in the event that it is handed down.

3. Consider starting your letter with either your benefit statement or a testimonial from a former employer.

4. Use bullet format to briefly list your top three accomplishments. You want your introductory letter to be only one page in length. This brevity will increase the likelihood that someone will actually take the time to read it.

Remember that you have to communicate to your reader in some way how you are going to solve a problem for them that are not currently being resolved and/or what value you bring to the organization.

Show them how you can save them money, make them money, or solve a problem that is not currently being resolved.

5. End your letter by thanking the hiring authority for their time and telling them that you will call them either later in the week. In the case of a letter that you know they will receive on Tuesday, stipulate that you will contact them Thursday at 9:15 A.M. When you give a specific day and time, it demonstrates the level of your commitment to follow up and shows that you are serious. Call/ follow up with your prospects when you say you are going to.

   Continue to follow up until you connect with the person, but be careful not to become a pest. Pay special attention to pacing and spacing your follow-up attempts. Try different techniques such as phone, email, and fax. Remember that their sense of urgency is not the same as yours.

By the third week, see if you can find some article online, in a newspaper, or in a magazine that you feel would be of interest to the person you are reaching out to. Send that article to them with a short note attached telling them you thought of them when you saw the article. Add that you thought they might find it of interest. Hand-write your note in legible blue ink. Include one of your business cards in addition to having your contact information on your letterhead. Tell them you plan to give them a call next Tuesday. Then call them on the day (date) you have mentioned. Hand-address the envelope with blue ink and an American flag stamp.

6. If you do not connect with someone, don't take it personally. For some reason, I have found that what used to be considered normal business courtesy—at least returning a phone call—does not seem to be a standard one in today's world.

To some degree, it is still a numbers game. Eventually you'll have the luck of suddenly finding yourself in the right place, at the right time, with the right business background.

7. Get back to basics. Don't be surprised if it takes you 20 to 30 phone calls to get one interview.

Remember that the majority of the jobs are in the hidden job market and in this current market most are being found and filled through networking.

That is why you target company lists will become the backbone to your success in your job search campaign.

I recommend that you try the Target Company Profile system I have suggested in this chapter. Why? Studies show that 3% of all job seekers connect with the target companies they mail or email.

Furthermore, 80% of the job seekers who follow up on their networking efforts after their initial mailing succeed in connecting.

In an earlier chapter, I mentioned that most people do not follow up and follow through! If you do so, you will increase your success rates in all areas of your job search. Follow-up is one of the secret weapons that give you a competitive edge.

*We will either find a way, or make one.*
—Hannibal

## Job Search Expert Action Plan

1 Use the "Target Company Profile Checklist" to help you fill in your Excel spreadsheet.

2 Use from your reader Bonus Material, "Job Search Experts Company Tracking Form." This is a form that should be modified for both your target company and

networking research. Save different versions (e.g., different industries, SIC codes, cities, etc.).

3 Create different forms for your target "A," "B," "Maybe," and "Discard" lists.

4 This Excel spreadsheet will be one of the primary work horses of your job search.

## Additional Job Search Notes

CHAPTER **8**

# Powerful Networking Strategies and Techniques That Work!

*A man, sir, must keep his friendships in
constant repair. If a man does not make
new acquaintances as he advances through
life, he will soon find himself left alone.*

—SAMUEL JOHNSON

## The Intense Power of Networking in Your Job Search

THIS IS THE ESSENCE of good networking: Work on staying in touch with your professional and personal contacts on a regular basis, not just when you need their help like when you're looking for a job. Ideally you do not want to find yourself unemployed and suddenly having to start from scratch in building your network.

I realize that when we are working, we can get busy in our day-to-day business. As a result, sometimes we do not find the time to stay in touch with the people with whom we have developed business and personal relationships with over time. That blasé attitude, however, is a mistake. We need to slow down and get back to connecting with people in a genuine way.

In study after study, networking is consistently cited as the number one way to get a job. According to CareerXRoads' 10th Annual Sources of Hire Study (March 2011), "referrals make up 27.5% of all external hires." This figure represents an increase over 2009's referral number of 26.7% (new employees hired from outside the organization). Compare this to the percentage of hires made as a result of postings on job boards in 2010 (24.9% of external hires) and you begin to see just how important networking is.

Networking is like one big scavenger hunt. At the outset, you have no idea where it will ultimately take you. At times, the path will not seem obvious, but whatever you do, don't become complacent and stop networking. Keep following the clues until you land the job!

Fortunately, here are a lot of clues to keep you engaged in networking. Never prejudge a clue (or contact) because you never know where or, more importantly, who it will lead you to.

A vast amount of resources exist on the internet that you can use for your networking. In addition you have all the books that have been written on the topic you can consult.

It's important to keep in mind that approximately 90% of executive job placements are found in the hidden job market. More importantly, the most efficient way to tap into that hidden job market is to utilize networking techniques.

People you will be networking with will primarily fall into three categories:

1. Those people you already know personally and professionally (A)

2. Those people your current personal and professional contacts know and the people to whom they may be able to refer you (B)

3. Those people you are aware of but whom you and your current contacts do not currently know personally—These

individuals will predominantly exist in your target companies. (C)

When it comes to networking, three seems to be the magic number. There are also three levels of job search networking leads.

1. People who will provide you with helpful information and advice

2. People who will be able to refer you to a company and an internal employee

3. People who will know the actual hiring authority or supervisor for a position in the department you would like to work in—(Leveraging such an opportunity assumes you have the correct professional background for the company, department, and position.)

Some basic rules apply to networking that remain the same regardless of the situation and approach you are using.

### 8-Step Unbeatable Networking System

1. **Networking Tools**—From the start, create a way to track and update all your networking leads and connections. You will be able to use your Excel spreadsheet from Chapter 7 by modifying it for the networking portion of your job search.

    In addition to this spreadsheet, you can also create a separate "New Contact Group" in you Microsoft Outlook program specifically for your networking contacts.

2. **Who Do You Know?**—Create a list of all the people you know with whom you can network both personally and professionally. Leave no one off the list!

3. **What Organizations Are You Aware Of?**—Create a list of all the organizations (e.g., church, college alumni,

industry associations, school directory, etc.) you are aware of where you can network.

4. **Research**—Do your research in advance on the companies and the people you plan to network with. Create a list of 50 target companies/people. Prioritize them into A (20), B, and C categories.


When you are researching the companies you are interested in, see if you can uncover a problem or need they have that your professional background and expertise can help solve.

Look on the internet for articles in the *Wall Street Journal*, industry publications, etc. to help with this research.

**Organizations hire people to solve a problem within their company that is not currently being resolved.**

You must ask yourself, "Where can I add value with my accomplishments?" That is the key!

You need to discover what problem(s) your targeted companies need solved and, if at all possible, how much that problem is costing them in terms of lost sales and revenues.

This information may not be easy to root out, but if you succeed, you have put yourself in a stronger situation going into your meeting. I can't say it strongly enough: research, research, research . . . and then research some more. Have I made myself clear on this issue?

Once you have figured out how you can help the organization you are applying to, you will need to develop a seven-second benefit statement. Then, when you are in the hiring authority's presence, you will be able to share that statement with them.

The greater the value you bring to a hidden employer with respect to solving a problem, the higher the probability you will get hired by them. You must be fully prepared with this knowledge prior to networking with your contacts.

How do you arm yourself with this vital information? Go directly to the company's website, to Hoovers, and to the other sources found in your local library that we discussed in previous chapters. (See "Target Companies" chapter.)

Don't forget that you can also use Google: www.google.com .au/advanced_search. Following are some tips on how to best leverage this search engine in your networking efforts:

1) Type the *full* name of the company you want to research in the top line that is labeled "all these words" (e.g., ABC Resume).

2) In the second line, "this exact wording or phrase," type "work experience."

3) Skip the next line and go to "any of these unwanted words." Type "applies" or "apply."

Look for a company among the returned links from your search results. This will help you uncover leads to previous employees from the company you are interested in contacting in addition to job leads within the organization. With any bit of luck, you will also find phone numbers.

Another technique entails using Google "Advanced Search" to research people and gain more information about them:

1) Type the name of the company in the first line.

2) On the third line down, type the title of the person two levels up to whom you would be reporting (e.g., "vice president of sales").

3) On the fourth line, type "free." Then refine your search again using Google "Advanced Search."
   a) In the top box/line, enter the first and last name of the person.
   b) On the third line, enter the company name.
   c) Press "Advanced Search" for your results.

You can also look up individual's profiles at:

- www.LinkedIn.com
- www.Facebook.com
- www.Ryze.com
- www.Friendster.com
- www.Spoke.com
- www.Classmates.com
- www.ZoomInfo.com

With all these methods, see if you can uncover any interests you have in common with your potential contacts. You can use this point of commonality to start building a relationship with them.

Above all else, you must come off and appear genuine and authentic when reaching out to a new contact. You need to show them you care about them as an individual. That said, try to find a way in which you will be able to help them and add value to their life.

Remember that people help and hire individuals they feel comfortable with, like, and trust. This is the all-important "know, like, and trust" principle that applies to the job search process. Members of your network need to get to know you in some small way to start building the "know" portion of this equation. That way, they can begin to like you and trust you. Then they feel as though you are credible and "believable."

> *Do not go where the path may lead;*
> *go instead where there is no path and leave a trail.*
> —Ralph Waldo Emerson

5. **Setting Up a Networking Meeting**—Following is some suggested dialogue for getting a networking meeting set up.

   *Hi, Mr. Smith, this is Eleanor Sweet. Do you have a real quick minute or have I caught you at a bad time?*

This opener sets the tone by showing you respect the person you are speaking with and their time. From the get-go, you establish that you're interested in them and not just yourself.

Ask them for 15 to 20 minutes of their time. Be upfront that you are hoping they can introduce you to people who might be able to provide advice.

> *I just want you to know that I do not expect a job, a position, or a favor of any kind. I have learned that you know a lot about this industry/product category and job market. I am hoping you could provide me with some helpful information. I would appreciate that very much.*
>
> *Would you be able to give me 15 to 20 minutes tomorrow morning around 8:15 A.M.? Or Wednesday afternoon around 1:15 P.M.?*

Listen; do not interrupt. Notice that you are offering an alternate time from the first one. By doing so, you are subtly asking your contact to choose one of the two times. This approach increases your odds for getting a "meeting" commitment.

Make sure you're the last one to hang up the phone at the end of the conversation. By hanging up last, you are leaving the caller with a good feeling about both you and the call. Then call the day before the meeting to confirm.

6. **The Meeting**—Get to the meeting 10 minutes early. Do not stay beyond the timeframe you initially set up.

Again, do not ask for a job. If a problem is mentioned during your meeting that you can solve, casually mention what you can do that will benefit the company relative to that problem. Then back off from the situation. (You can reiterate your benefit and value in your thank-you letter.)

You can also use the following verbiage in your meeting.

*Is there someone perhaps I have not thought of you think I should be networking with who might be able to help me?*

*May I use your name?*

Again, this comment expresses your respect for the individual and their relationship with you.

Keep track of honoring the time commitment you have set up. If they ask you to stay beyond the specified time period, that is fine . . . but only if they are doing the asking.

Most importantly, you want to show your networking contacts that you respect their time and that you honor your commitments. You do not want to run over the time allotted for the meeting.

Prior to leaving, ask them, "Is there anything I can do for you?" Find out if they have any needs of ANY kind with which you might be able to help. You want them to know you care about them as a person. You don't want to leave the impression that you are just taking job lead ideas for yourself.

People tend to like people who help them. As such, they will make more of an effort to help those individuals they like. By helping them first, you are subtly persuading people to help you.

Once you've established a basic level of camaraderie, tell them you would like to send them a copy of your resume to have on file. Don't be presumptuous. Ask them if that would be all right. If they say yes, ask them if they would prefer to receive it via email, mail, or fax.

Mention that you will keep them informed of the results that arise from your job search. This is a subtle way to keep the door open and to continue building both the relationship and the acceptability to call them again.

Before you part ways, thank your contact verbally for their time and for any ideas they may have given you.

Abraham Lincoln said, "If you want to win a man to your cause, you must first convince him you are his friend."

Bob Burg has graciously allowed me to share with you his list of "10 Feel-Good Questions®". The list will provide you with additional ideas for questions you can use and modify for your job search. Realistically you will only be able to ask a couple of these questions while you are networking. You will find it as part of your reader Bonus Materials that you downloaded.

Bob Burg is the author of *Endless Referrals* and coauthor of *The Go-Giver* and *Go-Givers Sell More*. The list of questions is from his book, *Endless Referrals*.

7. **Thank-You Follow-Up**—Follow up with your contact immediately following your encounter to thank them for their time once again. Tell them how much they helped you, referring to the specific information that you found helpful.

A handwritten thank you is better than an email. It will stand out as being more personalized. If your handwriting is really bad, type it, print it, and then sign it by hand. Studies have shown that blue ink makes more of an impression.

Include a resume if you did not give your contact one during your networking/informational meeting. Based on the information you gathered in your informational interview, you can now customize your resume and thank-you letter to fit their culture and job needs.

Emailed thank-you notes are more appropriate for the traditional interview process.

In closing, remember to state exactly what benefit and value you can add to the organization in solving their problem. Remember, organizations hire people who can solve problems.

8. **Second Follow-Up**—Send a second handwritten thank-you note after you have officially met with the person your

initial contact referred you to. Thank them for the referral and give them an update on how the meeting went. Do this about two to three weeks after your initial meeting.

Now would be a good time to send a copy of a relevant article, some information on a competitor, or a piece of industry news you have uncovered that you think would be of interest to your contact.

Also, if there is a business book you have read that you believe pertains to topics that came up in your conversation with them; supply them with its information.

Now that you reached out a second time, keep following up at regular intervals.

> *It's not whether you get knocked down;*
> *it's whether you get up.*
> —Vince Lombardi

Don't get discouraged. Keep networking and keep trying. Networking is like growing a garden. At first it appears like nothing is happening, but then the flowers slowly start to come up.

The trick is that you have to keep an eye on your garden. You must keep watering the plants so they do not die.

While in your last position, I suspect some of you forgot to "water" your network. As a result, it will be a bit slower for you in the beginning of your job search than it will be for those of you who have stayed current with your professional network.

If you fall into the former category, let it be a strong lesson learned. Always stay in touch with your network in some small way. And don't be afraid to reach out at times to help others. As with life, what goes around comes around.

Remember to be genuine throughout this entire networking process. People will sense if you are not being authentic. They will not be eager to help you if they think you're being untruthful, insincere, and disingenuous about caring about them.

People land jobs by creating effective networking job leads that can provide introductions to hiring authorities.

## How to Use Social Media with Your Job Search Networking

The jury is still out on how much of a powerhouse Social Media will become in terms of company referrals. Nonetheless, I would like to share a success story on that front.

There was an assistant webmaster that, while unemployed, landed his job via Twitter by hitting upon a creative idea using Twitter Search. What he did was enter key phrases such as hiring Social Media, Social Media jobs, online community manager, blogging jobs, etc.

He then pulled the RSS feeds of these keyword conversations into Google Reader and made a habit of checking them first thing in the morning every day. If he came across conversations related to his keywords and they sounded like a good fit for him, he took the liberty of introducing himself via Twitter. Most times, the open jobs he inquired about had not been officially posted. Over time, in this way, he landed his job.

Welcome to Job Search 4.0 era. It is a new age indeed.

## 6 Tips on How to Use LinkedIn for Job Search Networking

1. You can use LinkedIn's search tools to find executives who are in your target companies. In the search bar, choose the "Companies" option and enter the name of the company you're interested in contacting. Under the industry section, pick "Any Industry" or the specific one you prefer. You will then be presented with a list of LinkedIn members who work for that company.

2. Go to the "Companies" tab and try this technique. Select "Browse All Industries" and select your industry. Look at every profile that interests you. When you have the profiles open, look at which "Groups and Associations" they have listed. This is another area to look for in your

networking endeavors. If it makes sense, join the same group.

3. Consider joining Toplinked at www.toplinked.com. You should be able to link to its members. This group is made up of "open networkers" in LinkedIn who should be fairly amenable to accepting your invitation.

4. Make sure you are working on getting LinkedIn recommendations from your past supervisors, customers, peers, etc.

5. Don't forget to look at the "Applications" link on your LinkedIn home page. Check out which applications you would like to add to your account.

6. Consider adding the "Polls" function, which allows you to send a poll about your job search to your list. You will need to have 150 contacts in order to be able to use this product, but you will be able to reach everyone faster than by emailing or phoning them.

There are various products out there that will coordinate and connect all your Social Networking sites for you. Linking them all together will save you time. That's because everything will be updated at the same time. Not only is it a competitive market out there, but it's also constantly changing technologically. That being the case, anything you can do to simplify the process is beneficial.

### Additional Job Search Networking Ideas

Another different idea is to check out www.networkingfor professionals.com.

This is an organization that sets up live after-hour networking meetings in the New York Tristate area, Arizona, Florida, Georgia, California, Illinois, Massachusetts, Pennsylvania, and Texas. If you live in those states, there is a membership fee as well as a fee for attending events. If you do not live in those states, then you get a free membership.

Another idea is to check out the following websites:

- www.yahoo.com/groups
- www.vault.com
- www.aol.com
- www.lycos.com

The University of Texas has also created a list of all the colleges and universities that is available online at www.utexas .edu/world/univ/alpha/. This can be a great tool to do alumni searches.

In closing, there are a lot of different ways to network. You should attend networking groups, call your network contacts, and try to "meet" and talk to as many people as possible.

Do not stop filling your pipeline with leads. Your job search can change overnight either way. You want to keep trying all methods. You never know where one contact, lead, or phone call will take you.

There is no single guaranteed path to success. In this competitive market, you are the one who has to be proactive. Go the extra mile and it will pay off for you. Never stop until you land the job!

> *The first one gets the oyster,*
> *the second one get the shell.*
> —Andrew Carnegie

## Job Search Expert Action Plan

1 Find out where all your past supervisors are and contact them over the phone. Since you will most likely be asking them to be professional references, I cannot stress enough

the importance of reaching out to them in person or over the phone. Use email or LinkedIn only as a last resort.

2   Make it point to reach out every day to people personally and professionally with whom you have lost touch.

3   Once you have touched base with someone, send them a handwritten note telling them how much you have appreciated catching up with them.

# CHAPTER 9

# Hidden Job Market Tools

## Creative Job Search Ideas: Informational Interviews and Broadcast Letters

*The more extensive a man's knowledge*
*of what has been done, the greater will*
*be his power of knowing what to do.*

—BENJAMIN DISRAELI

### Land of Opportunity—Jobs!

AS WE DISCUSSED in a previous chapter, CareerXRoads 10th Annual Sources of Hire Study (March 2011) deemed networking the number one way to find a job. In fact, referrals make up 27.5% of all external hires (new employees hired from outside the organization), while job boards represent only 24.9% of external hires.

Indeed, approximately 80% of all executive job placements are currently found in the hidden job market. (As a comparison, according to author Michael Farr in *Getting the Job You Really Want*, in 2007 that number was 65%.) The question becomes, how do you tap into that hidden job market? The most efficient way is to utilize various networking techniques.

In this chapter, we will examine two creative techniques cracking the hidden job market code: the informational interview and the broadcast letter technique.

### Informational Meetings—Hidden Strengths

First, let's talk about what some people call the informational interview. Personally, I prefer the term informational meeting, but the two terms mean the same thing. I simply find the latter name lower key and more representative of what is actually trying to be accomplished. In my opinion, informational interview sounds a little more structured and even stressful than the type of meeting you want to take place.

An informational meeting is just like it sounds: one you arrange in order to collect information about a job, career field, industry, or company.

As previously discussed, as part of the personal networking portion of your job search campaign, you should be contacting 25 to 30 people daily. If you're doing that, realistically speaking, you will only be able to make 50 to 100 follow-up calls a week. Plan for more calls than you think you will make, and you may just find yourself achieving a greater number of follow-ups than you thought you were capable of. Set the goal high and you'll soar higher than you initially believed! Remember the key is the sooner you get through your "no's" the sooner you will uncover your "yeses."

Relative to your target companies, you should be working on networking with your 25 to 50 (35) "A" companies on a daily basis. You should also plan to have 50 to 75 companies on your "B" companies list and 75 to 125 on you "C" list.

Because most job seekers will not use these techniques, this will give you an edge in uncovering the hidden jobs others are virtually ignoring. Leverage your target company lists to unearth the hidden jobs no one is going after!

At this point, you're probably asking, "If they need a job and are looking for a new one, why are most people not trying this strategy?" The answer is that the techniques I'm suggesting here are designed for the truly motivated and committed job seekers who want to win the job! They involve hard work and consistent effort on your part, something not everyone wants to put into their job search.

That said, conducting a job search campaign in the hidden job market can, at times, prove more challenging. One of the reasons it is more difficult is that you find yourself more on the front line, where the likelihood of being rejected is much higher. Prior to this economy, the typical rejection rate was 20–30% of every 100 letters sent out. In this current market, that number is more likely to be 40%–60%. Now compare that to the typical success record, which can run about 2–4% depending on your situation, and the fear associated with the hidden job market is warranted.

But don't forget that the faster you get through the "no's" the faster you get to the homerun "yes." The name of the game is persistence. At times, staying in the job search game may require a higher level of persistence than you're used to. Over time, the lack of seeing results may begin to wear on you. Don't let them beat you! The results you're seeking are just around the corner, so hang in there.

As you continue to push forward, here are some points to ponder:

*The next mile is the only one a person really has to make.*
—Danish proverb

*The rewards for those who persevere far exceed*
*the pain that must precede the victory.*
—Ted Engstrom

With both of the techniques that are the focus of this chapter (informational interviews and broadcast letters), you *will* succeed. It's just a matter of time. I know this to be true in my heart, and I personally have achieved professional success with both of these strategies prior to becoming a recruiter.

Remember that the urge to quit will tend to creep in. You will have to be firm with yourself and stay the course. Most people say they are committed but really they lack the level of devotion and drive that is needed to truly succeed.

Neither the informational meeting nor the broadcast letter technique necessarily requires more skill or talent. What you do need to make them succeed is more guts, more strength of heart, more stamina, more discipline, and more personal commitment. The key lies in adopting the attitude *Veni, Vini, Vici*: I came, I saw, I conquered.

The informational meeting technique is especially useful in these three situations:

1. Traditionally, the informational interview had its roots with those individuals who were graduating college and just entering their career. If you're entering your first job, the informational meeting can be invaluable. The informational interview is also a very effective tool for those career changers who are considering a new and different career path. It is an excellent way to obtain some insight into what is required of a new position and how realistic it is for you to consider that position as your next viable career move.

2. The informational meeting is a secret weapon that most people who are currently in the job market would not think to use. Because you will be one of the limited few job seekers leveraging it, you will enjoy a competitive edge over the competition.

In all cases, the informational interview just makes logical sense. Talking firsthand to the people who are in the trenches will help you get the inside scoop.

But new graduates and career changers aren't the only ones who will benefit from the informational meeting. The technique is also good for those individuals who are currently in the job market who are hoping to stay in their current professional area of expertise and/or industry. That is because it forces you to get yourself out in front of your industry's executives.

As a result, you suddenly become a real person in their eyes. Any time you can visibly position yourself as more of a live human being, you gain an edge over the person who is seen as just a piece of paper. It all comes back to the fact that people always want to hire and help those whom they know, like, and trust.

This is another reason why networking is so effective. The more you are a real person the more others will make that extra effort to help you. It is also harder to say no to a person with whom a hiring authority has some type of pre-established relationship with than it is to reject someone they have never personally met.

In addition, by nature, people genuinely like to help other people. Remember that.

### How to Get Started Using This Technique

To get started on this technique, I suggest you create an Excel spreadsheet marked "Prospective Informational Meetings." Move that spreadsheet to the front burner, at the top of your Five Daily Goals list.

As we previously discussed, the networking portion of your job search campaign should consist of contacting 25 to 30 people daily. Relative to your target companies, on a daily basis, you should be working on networking with your to 25 to 50 "A" companies and 50 to 75 "B" companies.

From your list of networking contacts and target companies, select those that are in your industry (or an aligned industry) and that are located within a realistic geographical area (i.e., one that is close enough to drive to and get a face-to-face meeting with the hiring authority).

Now pick the first 10 contacts/companies on that list and conduct enough initial research into them to confirm in your mind that at this time, with the limited information at your disposal, it makes sense for you to take things to the next level (i.e., trying to set up an informational meeting). Research your targeted organizations for the names of the internal employees you will be contacting if you are unable to find a referral from the outside. Once you feel as though you have a good understanding of the contact/organization, you are ready to make the call and set up an informational meeting.

Start "working" the list. See if you can find someone you know who can act as a referral at each organization you're targeting. If that is not possible, then spend some time researching and validating a possible contact whose title is two levels above the one you would be working at.

You want to avoid contacting someone who is at your level or your boss's level, lest you end up intimidating them. You need to be contacting someone who 1) will not be intimated by you, 2) is in a position to hire you, and 3) is knowledgeable about the organization and industry at large.

Make achieving an informational meeting with this list of contacts and companies your goal within in the next 30 days. (Do not forget to include competitors of your past employers on this list.) My suggestion is to research your 10 contact/companies and then make the 10 phone calls that will land you informational meetings with them.

Realistically you will not usually get through on the first try. It may take several attempts. I would say to call on a Monday, Wednesday, or Friday. Most people who travel are not as likely to be on the road on Mondays and Fridays. I would also suggest calling around 8:15 A.M., 11:40 A.M., 1:10 P.M., 4:35 P.M., or 5:10 P.M. Other times should work, but historically speaking, it is during these timeframes that I have found it easier to catch people whose schedules I was not familiar with.

## Setting Up an Informational Meeting

Remember that when you're setting up an informational meeting you're simply seeking information. You are in control of the meeting because you're the one asking all the questions.

Ideally, as a result of your meeting, you hope to uncover either some problem the company has that you can solve or a future employment opportunity.

Employers will generally consent to an informational meeting if they feel as though they can trust you not to hound them for a job. You need to make this fact clear to them over the phone when you call to request your meeting.

I suggest you try to set up your informational meeting over the phone first. As a fallback, you can do so via email or snail mail, but only as a secondary approach. The reason is that you are able to build more of a relationship over the phone than you can through an impersonal piece of correspondence. The more visible you make yourself as a person the more you work the job search process to your benefit.

Following is an example of the type of dialogue you can modify when reaching out for an informational interview via phone:

> *Hello, Mr. Hawkins, my name is Eleanor Sweet. Do you have a real quick minute, or have I caught you at a bad time?* (If you have the name of a referral, now would be the time to mention it.)

This verbiage sets the tone of the conversation by showing you respect the individual and their time. You establish that you are interested in them and not just yourself.

> *I just want you to know that I do not expect a job, a position, or a favor of any kind. I have learned that you know a lot about this industry/product area/area of expertise and job market. I am hoping you can*

*provide me with some helpful information. I would appreciate that very much.*

*Would you be able to give me 15 to 20 minutes tomorrow morning around 8:15 A.M.? Or Wednesday afternoon around 1:15 P.M.?*

Listen; do not interrupt. Also, make sure you are the last one to hang up the phone at the end of the conversation. It sets a subtle tone of courtesy if you hang up last.

Now that you've secured a meeting, go out and conduct more in-depth research on the organization you'll be interviewing with. You need to be prepared for your meeting. If you can, go out and physically see the company's product, do some store checks, and/or locate the firm's customers.

When you are fully informed about the company you're interviewing with, you'll come across as more intelligent and professional. Your answers will be more informed because you've done your homework. You will not be wasting your interview partner's time with dumb questions.

### Actual Informational Meeting

Following are some tips to ensure your informational interview goes smoothly.

1. Call the day of the meeting to confirm it.

2. Get to the meeting 10 minutes early. Do not stay longer than the time you have set up for it. Realistically, the meeting will last about 30 minutes.

3. Again, and I can't stress this enough, do not ask for a job. If a problem is mentioned during your meeting that you can solve, casually mention what you can do that will benefit the company relative to it. Then back off from the situation. (You can reiterate your benefit and value in your thank-you letter.)

4. Keep track of honoring the timeslot you committed to. When the allotted time is up (15–20 minutes), thank your interview partner for their time and prepare to leave. If they ask you to stay beyond the designated timeslot, that is fine, but only if they are inviting you to linger. Most importantly, you want to show them that you respect their time and honor your commitments.

5. Ask them if there are any people they think you should contact for additional information and assistance. Try these segues:
   - "Do you know of anyone who might have a job opening in my field?" (If no, then . . .)
   - "Do you know of anyone who might know of someone who would?" (If no then . . .)
   - "Do you know someone who knows a lot of people in the industry whom you think I should talk to?"

6. Prior to leaving, ask, "Is there anything I can do for you?" or
   "What can I do to help you?"

7. Tell the person you've met with that you would like to send them a copy of your resume to have on file. Ask them if they would prefer to receive it via email, mail, or fax.

8. Mention that you will keep them informed on the results of your search. This is a subtle way to keep the door open and continue to build the relationship.

9. Thank your interview partner verbally for their time and for any ideas they were able to share with you. Make sure you exchange business cards.

10. When you return home, remember to update your notes on the company in your Excel spreadsheet. Include any job leads or ideas you picked up during the meeting that you need to follow up on.

## Guidelines for Your Follow-Up Letters

Follow up immediately (within 24 to 48 hours) after your meeting to thank the person you've spoken with for their time. Tell them how much they helped you, and as a personal touch, refer to some specific information they shared with you that you found helpful.

A handwritten thank-you letter is better than an email. It will stand out as being more personalized. If your handwriting is really bad, type it, print it out, and sign it by hand.

Include a resume if you did not give the individual one during your meeting.

Also, remember to state exactly what benefit and value you can add to the organization in solving their problems. The information you uncovered through your research or via your meeting will come in handy here.

Follow up again in two to three weeks with some article or industry information you think will interest the person you met with. Stay in touch and keep the lines of commutation open. Also, keep the contact posted on your job search's progress.

I personally used this technique when I was graduating college and wanted to land a job in an advertising agency. I was able to set up four to five informational meetings on a single trip to New York City. I found these meetings so informative, in fact, that I decided I did not want to pursue a career path than involved working for an advertising agency.

## Secret Weapon—Broadcast Letter

Now I would like to switch gears to talk about the broadcast letter. This is a job search technique I'm a keen believer in. In fact, a broadcast letter is how I got my marketing job with Salton. I had recently moved to Chicago because of my marriage, having previously been with GE Lighting. I wanted to transition from national accounts manager to marketing. As is to be expected, it's hard to make a career transition to a different area where you have no proven track record. This is true, even though you *think* you can make the transition.

The broadcast letter is particularly effective for:

1. People who have had multiple job changes (fewer than two years per job)

2. People who are 45+ years old

3. People who are considering a career change in terms of either industry, product category, or primary professional expertise (such as myself in the aforementioned example)

A broadcast letter is a hybrid between a cover letter and a resume. Unlike a resume, however, which is more about a call of action, a broadcast letter is more about branding.

In situations like those mentioned above, instead of sending a resume, you send your broadcast letter. The good thing about broadcast letters is that they can generate leads for you. That's because all companies have problems that need to be solved. It's all a matter of chance as to whether it's the right time for someone with your type of background.

Address your broadcast letter to the president of the company you're targeting. By sending it to the top brass, your letter gets passed down to someone else and is less likely to be thrown away. That's because it's being routed from the president's office and therefore automatically deemed as important. Your letter will be more visible for two reasons: 1) it originated in the president's office and 2) you mailed a hard copy through the good old-fashioned mail.

In the reader Bonus Material for this chapter, I will provide a sample broadcast letter that you can use in your job search.

### How to Run a Broadcast Letter Campaign

To start with, I suggest an initial mailing to 100 to 200 company presidents. Create your list in Excel or any software where you will be able to do an easy mail merge. If you do not know how to do this yourself, find a friend to help you. Each week thereafter, mail 50 to 100 such letters. A goal of 500 will get you a high enough number of trees to shake to get the fruit to drop. When you mail 500 broadcast letters, you can expect to hear back from 3–5% of the recipients as being interested in your background.

Where do you get names to include on the list? Here are just a few starters:

1. Your local library or outplacement office

2. Poor's Register of Corporations, Directors and Executives

3. Dun & Bradstreet's "Million Dollar Directory"

4. Standard Register

5. Moody's Bank, Insurance, Real Estate, and Investment Trusts

6. Directory of Manufactures and Directory of Services

7. The Advertising Red Book

8. Hoover's

9. Trade Show Directories

10. Reference USA

By culling information from these sources, I am confident you will be able to find 100 to 200 companies in your geographical area that will be of interest to you.

The reason the broadcast letter strategy is so effective is that it puts the readers' focus on your generic accomplishments (quantifiable). It eliminates the tendency for them to initially filter you out because you are not from their industry, you are "too old," or you look like a job hopper. From your broadcast letter, they do not know any of that.

Basically you are whetting their appetite by impressing them with your accomplishments. The hope is that they will then call you to get further clarification on your background. Now you have a live person with whom you can engage in a dialogue.

I know it is faster and cheaper to use email, but you miss the opportunity to become a real person in the recipients' eyes. As a result, it is easier for them to screen you out via email.

Also, since there is no recruiter fee involved here, the recipient of your broadcast letter is more likely to take a risk on hiring you. That is because there is less at stake financially.

When you get an interview with someone on the basis of your broadcast letter, you will need to make sure they can see how your accomplishments and your problem-solving track record will translate to their organization. To up the likelihood of securing a fair number of such interviews, I suggest a goal of 65 to 70 broadcast letters per week.

### Writing Your Broadcast Letter

The broadcast letter should be one page and should get straight to the point.

1. Address the letter directly to the president of the company. Take the time to call to confirm that the same president is still there and that you have the correct spelling, title, and mailing address.

2. In the first paragraph, keep in mind that you are applying for the possibility of a job opening. As such, you want to address a problem that you can solve.

3. In the second paragraph, list some of your accomplishments in bullet format. Make sure they are generic rather than industry specific.

4. In the third paragraph, introduce your educational background or any additional skills that would be beneficial or relevant.

5. In the closing paragraph, tell the reader that you look forward to an opportunity to meet at their convenience. Then discuss any possibilities for such a meeting.

6. Thank the reader, expressing appreciation of their time and consideration.

7. If you think you can keep the commitment, you can also say that you will call the reader to follow up and answer any questions they might have. You can list the general timeframe, but you must be able to follow up and do what you say you will do.

I won't lie to you. The odds of the broadcast letter landing you a job are on the low side. For every 100 letters you send out, you should expect maybe five interviews.

Now you could say those odds aren't worth pursuing, but the method is like life. If you do not buy a lottery ticket, for instance, you will never even have a chance to win. You need to buy a ticket to have any opportunity to walk away with the jackpot!

My advice is to forget about the odds. Create your list, mail out your letters, and go for landing an interview!

This is a very competitive market. You never know where your next job will come from. You really have to give all available options a try to increase the odds of something fruitful shaking from the bushes.

I've personally had success with this method and know many other people who have as well. As I have mentioned before, most job searches have their challenges. In the case of this particular labor market, there are more challenges than usual. That being the case, you have to try more options to get those bushes shaking.

This is not a job market where you send five emails and land a job offer. Neither is this a market where you send five recruiters your resume and secure a job offer. Nor is this a job market where you answer five internet job postings and get a job.

In this extremely competitive market, the challenge lies in going where most people are not going. Be persistent, implement great follow-up, and differentiate yourself from the rest of the pack any way you can, and you *will* succeed.

As a final note on the subject of adversity, consider this quote:

*I have learned that success is to be measured not so much by the position that one has reached in life as by the obstacles which he has overcome while trying to succeed.*
—Booker T. Washington

## Job Search Expert Action Plan

1 Make sure you do plenty of research on the organizations and people you will be contacting for your informational interviews.

2 Remember to practice the suggested dialogue for setting up the informational meeting prior to calling your prospective contacts.

3 Send follow-up letters after each of your informational interviews.

4 Use your reader Bonus Material for this chapter, "Broadcast Letter Sample," to draft your own broadcast letter.

## Additional Job Search Notes

CHAPTER **10**

# Art of Marketing Yourself During Your Job Search

*There may be no single thing more important
in our efforts to achieve meaningful work
and fulfilling relationships than to learn
to practice the art of communication.*

—MAX DE PREE

IN THIS CHAPTER, the emphasis will be on the art of marketing yourself in your job search as well as personal branding. There are several ways in which you can accomplish these aims.

In the following pages, I will discuss ways to market yourself and create your personal brand. I will also help you develop your "elevator pitch" and your unique selling proposition (USP). In addition, I will offer some advice on using Social Media and your own personal blog as ways to market yourself.

### Creating Your Unique Selling Proposition (UPS)

First introduced in the 1940s by Rosser Reeves of Ted Bates and Company, the term unique selling proposition is today used in other fields. It is also tossed around casually to refer to **any aspect of an object that differentiates it from similar objects.**

In his book *Reality in Advertising*,[1] Reeves laments that the USP is widely misunderstood. He goes on to give a precise definition in three parts, as explained by Wikipedia:

1. Each advertisement must make a proposition to the consumer. It must not be just words, not just product *puffery*, not just show-window advertising. Each advertisement must say to every reader, "Buy this product, and you will get *this specific benefit*."

2. The proposition must be one that the competition either cannot or does not offer. It must be unique—either in the uniqueness of the brand or as a claim that is not otherwise made in that particular field of advertising.

3. The proposition must be so strong that it can move the mass millions (i.e., pull over new customers to your product).

Applying the Unique Selling Proposition method to the job search, your UPS should:

1. Tell the prospective employer, "Hire me and you will get this _____ benefit for your organization."

2. Pinpoint what you feel is unique about you and what you can bring to the organization. Alternatively, it should highlight something unique that can bring value to the company that other candidates cannot or are unable to communicate that they can.

---

[1] Reeves, *Reality in Advertising,* 1961, pp. 46–48

3. Showcase so strongly and compellingly the benefit and value you bring to the organization that the hiring authority is moved to hire you over all the other candidates they're considering.

This is the shortest of the marketing tools we will be discussing in this chapter. Basically your unique selling proposition should be kept to one sentence, two at the most. With your USP, you are stating how you are unique and different from all the other job candidates the hiring authority is considering.

When devising your proposition, ask yourself, "What is the most unique benefit or value I will bring to this organization?"

Once finalized, your USP is a versatile marketing tool. You can use your unique selling proposition verbally, in cover letters, and on your resume.

It is here where you "hook" your job contacts' interest enough that they reach out to you and ask you for more information. This is precisely what you're trying to do any time you use your UPS, either verbally or in writing. You want the person you're communicating with to engage with or connect with you. That is when you become more of a real person and you start to build a relationship with them.

People hire people they like and who can solve a problem that is currently not being resolved within their organization. Simply put, companies hire people who will either save them money or make them money!

That being the case, you want your major benefit here to be expressed in a quantifiable way—in other words in dollars saved, increased (sales) revenue, time saved that translated into money saved, or a major problem you solved that translated to increased money for your past employer.

Make sure you're comfortable with saying your unique selling proposition out loud. You want it to sound natural, like you, not like a robot.

## Your Job Search Elevator Pitch

The phrase "elevator pitch" comes from the hypothetical scenario in which you find yourself on an elevator with your dream employer and have only approximately 30 seconds to two minutes, the length of an average elevator ride, to sell yourself.

An elevator pitch is normally presented orally, but it can also be presented in writing or as a video. In a nutshell, it's a concise speech in which you provide the listener with an overview of your professional background and how you would bring value to their organization by solving a problem for them. (This listener could be someone you're networking with, a prospective employer, a prospective lead, etc.)

The goal in delivering your pitch is to remember to present your information concisely, clearly, and interestingly. You are selling yourself; you are "the brand."

You will have to gauge your audience in terms of how much time you will have to present. Start by creating a one-minute, 30-second, and 15-second version of your pitch. It will be easier to trim back for the shorter versions so begin with the longest one.

Follow these four simple steps to create your elevator pitch:

1. Introduce yourself. Briefly tell the listener who you are from a professional standpoint.

2. Next, state your value, phrased as key results or a major impact you would bring to the organization. This information should help your listener understand how you can add value to their organization.

3. Move on to talking about the unique benefits or skills you possess that you would bring to their organization. It's here where you differentiate yourself from other job seekers. Tell the listener how you're better than the other candidates who are vying for the same position. Be clear about why you're the best individual for their organization. Briefly discuss your top accomplishment. If you

have time, be prepared to introduce your second most impressive achievement.

4. Describe your immediate goals. Conclude with a forward-looking statement, such as, "I'm looking forward to the opportunity to . . ." or "I would like to know more about. . . ." The listener should know what you are asking of them.

As I've said numerous times throughout this book, companies hire a person who can solve a problem for them that is currently not being resolved. Ask yourself this question: "Where can I add value to the organization?" They are looking for people who can either save them money or make money for them. Keep this at the forefront of your mind when you write your elevator pitch.

Remember to practice, practice, practice. You need to have your elevator pitch memorized by heart for face-to-face meetings where it is appropriate to use it. At the same time, make sure the presentation of your elevator pitch is natural and authentic-sounding.

A tip to help you memorize it is to say the first line five times in a row. Then add the second sentence. Say that sentence five times. Then say the first and second sentence together five times. Keep repeating this process, adding the next sentence, until you have said the entire elevator pitch five times. Repeat this process every day until you have your pitch memorized.

If possible, videotape or record yourself giving your elevator pitch and then play back the tape. Don't lose heart. Practically no one gets it right the first time. Everyone must practice. Whenever possible, videotape yourself practicing your UPS and elevator pitch. Watching yourself in action and listening to your various speech patterns can be a real eye-opener.

Pay particular attention to your body language and posture. Listen to the tone and speed of your voice and how well you are clearly speaking (enunciating) during your pitch.

Keep a written copy of your elevator pitch near the phone. That way it will be easier, when appropriate, to present your sales pitch spur of the moment.

There is a great tool created by Harvard Business School (HBS) to help you build your elevator pitch. Go to www.alumni. hbs.edu/careers/pitch/.

HBS studies show that the average elevator pitch is 231 words in length.

They also tell us that the average pitch is 56 seconds long and has four repeated words in it.

Check your elevator pitch against the average pitch as a test to see if you need to edit yours so it is more in alignment with these suggested guidelines.

## Secrets to a Powerful Professional Summary

The professional summary is a marketing tool that is very effective for both networking and informational meetings.

Some of you who have participated in my weekly audio seminars will remember my feelings about sex and a resume. The same principle applies here. For those of you who were not with me on that audio, I suspect I caught your attention and you've now lifted your head out of your coffee mug.

The point here is that the odds are you didn't have sex with your husband or wife on your first date. The same is true with your resume. Less is better in the beginning. The more you share out of the gate, the faster the hiring authority will screen you out, particularly in this new economy. That's because they are overwhelmed with resumes from people who are looking for a new or better job. To combat this tendency, you want to share just enough information in your initial resume to get them wanting more information from you. You goal is to pique their interest enough that they set up a meeting with you.

In addition, I suggest you take that same philosophy and apply it to situations where you're marketing yourself at a networking event or during an informational meeting. In such scenarios, you would present your professional summary in lieu of your resume. You're trying to focus your contact's attention on you and what you bring of value to the table. After you have whetted their appetite or hooked them, you can then offer them your more complete resume.

When printing out your professional summary, it should be printed on the same paper stock you're using for your hard-copy resumes.

In creating your professional summary, at the top of the page put your name, address, phone number, and email. Then follow that information up with:

1. Summary—an overall short summary of your background. Finish this section with a one-sentence career objective.

2. Highlights—provide three to four career highlights.

3. Key personal and professional skills—three to four capabilities you think are important for the type of job you're seeking.

4. Achievements—highlight three to four past (quantifiable) career achievements.

**HINT:** The National Association of Colleges and Employers has surveyed employers for the last 10 years. In 2010, the 10 skills employers most wanted in an employee were:

1. Verbal and written communication skills

2. Honesty and integrity

3. Interpersonal skills

4. Teamwork skills

5. Strong work ethic

6. Motivation and initiative

7. Flexibility and adaptability

8. Computer skills

9. Analytical skills

10. Organizational skills

These qualities are all transferable soft skills employees use in every position, industry, and job. The good news is that if you're weak in some of these areas, you can practice and improve these sought-after skills on your own. You don't have to be currently employed to better yourself. You can increase these skills at home, with hobbies, in sports, and through everyday life experiences.

**6 Steps to a Strong Verbal Resume (Three to Four Minutes)**
The verbal resume is slightly different from the professional summary. First, it tends to be longer. Moreover, its primary basis is to serve as a shortened verbal version that highlights the key achievements on your resume.

Following is a suggested format for your verbal resume:

1. Devise a one- to two-sentence summary that is similar to your executive or career summary. (Try to avoid mentioning your career objective as it may give the listener a reason to screen you out at this point.)

2. Tell the listener where you were born and raised in one sentence. This strategy will make you become more of a person in their eyes. It also could lead to some natural dialogue, which will then have them interacting and connecting with you on a personal basis. Now you are starting to build a rapport and relationship with them.

3. Briefly (seven seconds) share with the listener your educational background. If you possess additional credentials or have completed classes that would be relevant to the job you are interviewing for, and then mention them.

4. Discuss your recent work experience. At this point, the bulk of your conversation should be relative to the most recent five to eight years of your professional history. Spend the majority of this time discussing your accomplishments from the past five to eight years. Don't waste time on anything further back in your career.

5. Share your current career status and the reason you left your past employer if you are currently unemployed. If you're looking to change companies, elaborate on the reason(s) why.

6. Tell the listener why you're attracted to their organization. Ask them if there are any areas of your background they would like additional information about.

### You are the Brand—How to Create "Your Brand" for Your Job Search

Branding comes in many forms. There's the type that encompasses individuals and organizations as the products to be branded. Then there's *personal branding* that treats persons and their careers as brands. The idea of personal branding really got its roots from an article titled "The Brand Called You," written by Tom Peters in 1997. There's also branding that treats the individual as the actual brand.

In defining personal branding, Peters tells us to "create a message and strategy to promote the brand called You." To accomplish this task, ask yourself:

- "What is it about me that makes me different from the other job seekers?" See if you can come up with an explanation that is 15 words or fewer.
- "What is my greatest and clearest strength?"
- "What is my most noteworthy personal trait?"

This is the old feature/benefit interplay at work here. What is a feature you possess that will have the most benefit for the employer?

Peters also says to ask yourself:

- "What do I do that adds remarkable, measurable, distinguished, and distinctive value?"
- "What do I do that I am most proud of?"
- "What have I accomplished that I can unabashedly brag about?"
- "Where have I added value that I can take credit for?"

The first step in any branding campaign is to increase visibility, and personal branding is no different. Think of ways you can become more visible in your job search. Everything matters in your personal visibility campaign, even the things you do not do.

Networking, or word-of-mouth marketing, is key in your job search personal branding campaign. Your network of friends, colleagues, clients, past employers, and customers is the most important marketing vehicle you have to drive your job search visibility. It's the hallmark of your personal brand.

You want the word out there that you are the type of person who makes major contributions to organizations. You want potential employers to view you as someone who is known to act like a credible leader.

Tom Peters has suggested that instead of using an old-fashioned resume, leverage the personal brand idea. Think instead in terms of a creating a marketing brochure for your brand: You.

He goes on to say, "You are a brand. You are in charge of your brand. There is no single path to success. And there is not one right way to create a brand called You. Except this: Start today, or else."

Another personal branding resource you may want to turn to is *BE Your Own Brand: Achieve More of What You Want by*

*Being More of Who You Are* by David McNally and Karl Speak. The book is good and comprehensive, addressing branding in a manner similar to a textbook approach.

In a nutshell, personal branding is very similar to your unique selling proposition. How do you differentiate yourself from others so that hiring authorities will trust you, find you believable, and be interested in contacting you to interview with their organization. The aim is to get them to want to get to know you, the brand, more.

Pick the skills you feel you excel in. Then match those skills up with your accomplishments. When integrating your personal brand into your cover letter and resume, *ask yourself the following questions about your accomplishments*. The answers will give you more valuable information to use to your advantage.

- Why?
- How?
- When?
- Who?
- What?

As I've mentioned before, try to quantify your accomplishments.

When at all possible, write your accomplishments in terms of concrete dollars or percent: dollars saved, increased sales dollars, increased revenue, the dollar value of time saved on a project, etc. Explain to the listener how you made the company money, saved them money, or increased their efficiency somewhere to the point that it resulted in an increased bottom line.

When you use your USP, elevator pitch, professional summary, verbal resume, and personal branding, you heighten and strengthen your visibility with a prospective employer.

The one thing you never want to be is generic in the eyes of the hiring authority. You want to position yourself as a solid standout, a unique star they want to get to know better and appreciate professionally.

**More Marketing and Branding Ideas for Your Job Search**

Another way to market and brand yourself in your job search is through the use of Social Media. Read closely the "Understanding the Power of Social Media" chapter of this book for more insight into this topic.

When you create your home page and profile on LinkedIn, Facebook, Twitter, or any other of the Social Networking sites, you are also creating your brand. These websites are great job search marketing tools.

That's the good news. The bad news is that you need to be careful of the type of information you put on these sites. Increasingly, employers and recruiters are visiting these sites to read up on you. That being the case, you want to make sure you keep the dialogue and pictures you post there more on the professional side. You also want to be consistent with the professional image you're trying to convey. Speaking of consistency, make sure all the information across all the Social Media platforms you're using is consistent and similar. For example, use the same picture on all platforms to maintain a consistent brand.

I'm also making the assumption here that everything being posted on your Social Media pages is authentic, genuine, and honest. Remember that the internet's history tends to linger, lasting much longer than most people realize it will endure. You need to make sure there's no misinformation on these sites relative to you and your background.

Also consider creating your own blog to get your personal brand out there for your job search. There are quite a few free blog sites available these days. Some examples worth looking into are www.blogger.com and www.WordPress.org. WordPress has made it relatively easy to blog and is by far the most popular blogging platform. For starters, go to the library and get WordPress for Dummies.

You can also create videos and post them on YouTube as part of your job search campaign. A word of caution, however:

Make sure you know what you're doing and that everything is very professional in terms of your content and visual image.

These videos should be approximately two to three minutes in length. At the end, give your name, phone number, email address, and personal website if applicable. This way, viewers will have a way to contact you.

You can also add these videos to your blog. Focus on presenting three to five of your best accomplishments. Describe your achievements without giving visitors the name of your past employers or industry. In addition, you can present your UPS or elevator pitch in another video. Tease visitors so they to want to contact you to gain more information about your professional background. The goal is that they will be so intrigued by what you've accomplished in the past that they'll be anxious to get someone like you on board in their organization.

I realize that most of you have not tried some of these techniques in your own personal job search. The key to a successful job search campaign, of course, lies in landing the job. To reach that aim, you need to stretch out of your personal comfort zone and try new ideas. You're looking for ways to differentiate yourself from the pack, the hordes of other people who are also looking for a job.

Remember that if you are currently employed, some of the techniques mentioned in this chapter will be appropriate, while others will be too visible for you to currently use in your job search while you are actively employed. If you're currently trying to keep your search for new employment under wraps, be selective and use common sense about which strategies you employ.

Some will tell you that the definition of insanity is continually doing the same thing over and over again without getting any results. We all need to change our direction at times to achieve success.

With this chapter, I challenge you to get out of your comfort zone and try some of these techniques. If you do, you should see an increase in the number of interviews you're landing compared to how many you had in the last 30 days.

> *Unless you try to do something beyond what you have already mastered, you will never grow.*
> —Ronald E. Osborn

> *If you don't have the power to change yourself, then nothing will change around you.*
> —Anwar Sadat

## Job Search Expert Action Plan

1 Use the HBS Elevator Pitch Builder by visiting:

www.alumni.hbs.edu/careers/pitch/.

2 Create your own mission statement by visiting Nightingale Conant at:

www.nightingale.com/mission_select.aspx

3 Use the Franklin Covey Mission Statement Builder by visiting:

www.franklincovey.com/msb/.

# CHAPTER 11

# Understanding and Using the Power of Social Media in Your Job Search

*The illiterate of the future will not be the person who cannot read. It will be the person who does not know how to learn.*

—Alvin Toffler

## Employers View of Social Media as a Hiring Tool

CAREERXROADS RECENTLY RELEASED their "10th Annual Source of Hire Report," written by Gerry Cruspin and Mark Mehler. This report focused on interviewing 36 organizations that, through various means, collectively filled 132,779 positions during 2010.

The study highlighted the 12 top external sources for hiring. Relative to Social Networking, two particular findings stood out from the rest. Social Networking falls primarily into the Direct-Sourcing area of external hiring. Direct-Sourcing ranked #5 at 5.0% of all external hires. This percentage and ranking is down from 2009 where direct sourcing ranked #4 at 6.9% of all external hiring.

What is certain is that Social Networking is included in Direct-Sourcing by 89% of the firms interviewed in the study. As part of their efforts to direct source candidates, 57% of Human Resource staff members either significantly or primarily research profiles on Social Networking sites such as LinkedIn, Facebook, etc.

In the event that an internal employee within the company refers a new hire they knew from LinkedIn, or some other Social Media source, that person is considered a "Referral" external hiring source. It should be noted that the study's sources do not break down what sub-portion of Referrals is attributable to Social Networking sites.

In a recent study of the Fortune 500 firms, CareerXRoads further noted that 45% of them have Social Media links embedded within their career website pages.

When you consider the impact that Social Media has on both the Direct-Sourcing and Referrals external hiring sources, you have to take notice. You can't ignore the fact that Social Media is another viable tool to understand and use with your job search.

A November 2009 study conducted by the Society of Human Resource Management (SHRM) illustrates this trend. Interviewing 75 companies, it specifically asked for a breakdown of the different types of Social Media they used.

More specifically, the study ranked how many of these companies were planning to try Social Media sources for their hiring needs in 2010. The results speak for themselves:

1. Facebook—75.4%

2. Official Company Blog—56.1%

3. LinkedIn—50.9%

4. YouTube—26.3%

5. Online Alumni Groups—26.3%

6. Alumni Social Networking Groups—12.3%

## Definitions

Before we dig any deeper, let's take a moment to cover some of the Social Networking vocabulary. One recent study of 600 people that is highlighted in *The Social Media Bible* asked, "What's the definition of 'Social Media'?" Interestingly enough, 70% of those questioned admitted they were not really familiar with the term.

In *The Social Media Bible: Tactics, Tools, and Strategies for Business Success*, authors Lon Safko and David Brake define the term this way: "Social media refers to activities, practices, and behaviors among communications of people who gather online to share information, knowledge, and opinions using conversational media."

Another way to look at the definition, as About.com guide Alison Doyle explains, is: "Social media includes various online technology tools that enable people to communicate easily via the internet to share information and resources. Social media can include text, audio, video, images, podcasts, and other multimedia communications."

Social Media can encompass:

1. Social networking sites

2. Reading a blog

3. Watching a YouTube video

4. Listening to a podcast

5. Sending a text message to another member of a community or group

Even more novel than Social Media is the phraseology Web 2.0, which it seems we are hearing about more and more these days. Turning to someone who's grown up in the age of Social

Networking, I asked my 14-year-old daughter what the definition of Web 2.0 was. She pretty much gave me the definition I'd been using prior to conducting in-depth research on this topic: In a nutshell, "Web 2.0 is the new and improved Web."

Based on Wikipedia, but simplified for this conversation, "The term Web 2.0 is commonly associated with web applications that facilitate interactive information-sharing and collaboration on the World Wide Web." It gives users the free choice to interact or collaborate with each other in a Social Media dialogue as creators of user-generated content in a viral community. Compare that to (Web 1.0) websites, where users are limited to passive viewing of content that was created for them.

The term Web 2.0 was created by Tim O'Reilly at a conference where he coined the phrase while serving as host. Loosely defined by most people, it refers to all the internet sites and tools that are all part of Social Media (e.g., blogs, social networking sites, "virtual" communities—anywhere someone interacts with others via the internet).

### 4 Styles of Social Media Approaches

This chapter will focus on some of the primary Social Media types you will encounter and will offer insight into how you can make sure you are maximizing these tools in your job search.

Social media is all about engaging your reader first. When approaching your audience, you have the option of:

1. Entertaining them

2. Collaborating with them

3. Communicating with them

4. Educating them

During your job search, you will traditionally experience the most impact with your contacts when you're communicating with and educating them through Social Media.

1. Entertain them—I hesitate to encourage the use of the first tool: entertaining your contacts. With the exception of someone who is specifically in the entertainment industry, I feel that very few people would be able to pull off this tool effectively and not, pardon my French, blow it.

   There is a tremendous risk of being misunderstood and considered highly unprofessional with trying the entertaining approach in your Social Media job search campaign. My professional advice is to stay away from this one unless you happen to be a professional entertainer.

   One of the primary rules in using any Social Media tools is to protect your personal and professional image. Better to play it safe in the entertainment department and not break that cardinal rule.

2. Collaborate with them—When you collaborate with your Social Media contacts (i.e., your audience), you're generally participating in an online discussion with them. This collaboration could take place in a chat room, in a LinkedIn group you are a member of, on a discussion board, or on Wikipedia, just to name a few.

   Notice that all of these places are ones where you can demonstrate that you are an expert in your industry, product category, channel of distribution, etc. Commenting on threads related to your areas of expertise is a subtle but powerful way to share and showcase your knowledge and skill.

   I suggest you monitor the discussion going on in a few groups for one to two weeks. Then pick the one you feel the most comfortable with in terms of your ability to add value to the conversation. Be sure to take your professional expertise relative to the majority of the topics discussed into consideration as well.

If you are currently employed, then focus on commenting when you are not at work. Plan to spend one to two hours a month taking part in Social Media collaboration.

If you are currently not employed and actively looking for a new job, then plan to spend either an hour a day or two hours every other day responding to your Social Media groups.

Unearthing networks to join is no problem. All the major Social Networking sites have discussion groups (e.g., LinkedIn's Groups Directory). You'll also find myriads to choose from at Yahoo Groups (groups.yahoo.com), Google Groups (groups.google.com), Ning.com, etc.

Be aware that it takes a lot of time to be actively involved in these discussion groups, but the effort can be well worth it. The payoff of increasing your visibility is one that can't be ignored.

When it comes to participation, always remember to be genuine, helpful, and truthful with your comments. You do not want to come across as desperate or begging for job assistance. You need fellow group members to view you as sincere. You want to come across as trying to add genuine value to the group discussion. Ideally, you'll be able to help someone else with your useful information.

**NOTE:** The next two methods of engaging your audience are the strongest approaches you can use in your job search.

3. Communicate with them—One of the most popular ways to engage your readers is to communicate with them. This may take the form of writing them an email, sending them a Twitter.com "Tweet," reaching out via Evite, Constant Contact, or Survey Monkey, or making use of any other Social Media applications.

The point here is that you are reaching out and networking with contacts that may be able to help you with your job search. This is where you want to engage your audience. You want to interact with your Social Networking contacts to:

a. Seek helpful information and advice from them. Ask them about companies and people they think will be helpful to your job search.

b. Get referred to a specific company or hiring authority within that company.

c. Connect with the actual person who would be your future boss.

4. Educate them about you and your professional background—This is where you would highlight a career background snapshot on your LinkedIn, Facebook, or Twitter profile page. These sites' profiles are an ideal place to showcase your mini pitch and professional branding.

Again, remember that less is better. You want to keep the information you highlight short and sweet, so that your contacts have to get in touch with you to obtain more information. Then you have succeeded in engaging them.

Also remember to ask them if there is any way you can help. I often see candidates who, while asking me for my help, graciously offer to return the favor by giving me access to their contacts for my own searches.

The goal here is to use these tools to educate others, be it friends, contacts, prospective employees, or anyone you can reach out to with which you can share your professional background.

## 16 Benefits of Social Networking in Job Search

*Why Participate in Social Networking?*

1. To expand your sphere of contacts

2. To expand your sphere of influence and exposure

3. To promote your professional brand

4. To leverage electronic networking

5. To find people who would otherwise be difficult to track down

6. To research people within your target companies

7. To more quickly get connected to the people who will help you with your search

8. To easily reach out and help others

9. To take advantage of job postings listed exclusively on the Social Networking sites

10. To draw attention to your mini professional bio

11. To fine-tune and perfect your elevator pitch

12. To come across as more of a real person (especially when you post a picture) than you would with just a resume

13. To connect with people in your industry

14. To connect with people in your career area

15. To connect with people in your geographical area

16. To join discussion groups and receive validation for quality information that demonstrates your expertise

### Practical Advice for Using Social Media during Your Job Search

Good tutorials can be found on most of the major Social Networking sites. In addition to doing these tutorials online, you might also want to go to the library and take out a very basic book such as *LinkedIn, Facebook*, or *Twitter for Dummies* or something similar.

When making a selection, make sure the language appears simple and straightforward. If you have a little patience, you should still be able to navigate the sites and get the hang of setting up and creating your profile there with a clear and easy-to-understand guidebook.

Over the course of researching this topic in depth, I found a real lack of quality books on the subject matter. For some reason, the books on Twitter seem to be the weakest of the three. That said, at this time, I'm not sure it would be worth it for you to actually purchase one.

In your reader Bonus Material for this chapter, you will find a list of suggested books to take out of your library on the topic Social Media.

Using Social Media, particularly Social Networking, can be intimidating for some people. It's like entering a hidden forest. At times, the technology appears to the novice to be a type of hidden etiquette that is not very obvious. With Social Networking you must employ subtle social skills.

Social Media, however, is one more tool you can use in your job search to help expand your sphere of contacts and, more importantly, your circle of influence. If you are just starting out, understand that Rome was not built in a day. You want to take your time as you rev up to speed. You will not necessarily achieve instant results. The important thing is that you will get results. Be patient.

### 20 Rules of Social Networking for Your Job Search

1. It is very important to be consistent with the information you post on all the Social Networking sites. (The same holds true for all other Social Media you use for your job search.)

2. Take your time, making sure you understand how each site works. (Again, check out the online tutorials, take

advantage of free webinars, and go to the library and get some very basic books.)

3. Make sure you are accurate with the information you post.

4. Make sure your information is succinct, so your contacts don't have to go searching for the details they need.

5. Remember to be yourself and to come across as genuine in all your conversations and postings.

6. Remember to reach out and help others.

7. Follow up and thank everyone who helps you.

8. Post a picture of yourself in your profile, assuming you have a fairly recent one that conveys a professional image. Remember to use the same photo on all of the Social Networking sites.

9. Before you connect with someone . . .
   a. Understand how they can help you.
   b. Understand how you can help them.
   c. Make sure you have something in common with them.
      It is better to have quality connections than to look like you are just running to win some race with the highest number. How can you possibly really know all those people enough to be able to genuinely help them?

10. Make an effort each day to try to find someone new to connect with. The connections of someone you already know are a good place to start.

11. Work on getting recommendations!!

12. On a daily basis, try to briefly communicate to everyone you're connected with any updates on your job search.

13. Each day, see if you can share a thought of the day, a quote, or some helpful information.

14. Never talk negatively about anyone you know or have worked with in the past on any of the social networks. If someone is asking your opinion about someone and it is not a favorable one, then call them in person and provide the information verbally.

15. The rule of thumb here is to use good old-fashioned common sense with a professional style.

16. Understand your privacy settings on all of the Social Networking sites.

17. Use your elevator pitch in your bio/profile section.

18. Follow the industry leaders.

19. Check all the job posting sections on all the sites.

20. In your email signature, remember to include your LinkedIn address link at the bottom. This will make it easy for people to connect with you there. Also, if you have a blog or website, remember to include those links at the bottom of your email signature as well.

### 10 Tips for Your Job Search Using LinkedIn

LinkedIn is still my favorite Social Media site. I have a bias toward it for a couple of reasons. The primary reason I like it the best is because I feel as though it has the strongest professional image. That is how it was originally set up and it does a good job of remaining true to that purpose.

The other reason I have a bias toward LinkedIn is that it was the first Social Networking site I joined.

A few things you might want to make sure you look into when joining LinkedIn:

1. Make sure you get recommendations. It's all part of the marketing and branding of you the person. I feel recommendations add a little pizzazz.

2. Make use of the feature where you can create a headline for yourself. I like this feature because, again, it is another way to continue to build your brand. Search "professional headline" for more information on this feature.

3. Look into creating your profile so you can include status updates. Updates are a great way to keep all your contacts posted on what's going on with your job search. They're also another way in which you can continue to come across as a real person by telling your story. The only rules are to keep your updates professional and brief.

4. Look into getting involved with LinkedIn Answers in addition to the other discussion groups you may be part of.

5. Don't forget to use the job search function at the top of the page marked Jobs. Click on the Find Jobs tab and then you should be able to conduct both basic and advanced searches.

   One of the neat things with LinkedIn is that it will show you how many degrees away you are from the person who posted the position. Once you click on the job title, you will be led to the job posting information. Then click on "Inside Connection to the Poster," which will give you detailed information on the individual who posted the job.

   Another option is to click on "Inside Connection to the Company." You will then see a list of people you know who are connected to the company advertising the job.

   You now have the option to submit an application directly via LinkedIn. In that case, request a referral to the job poster via the normal request process. The system will automatically set up the request for you and include a link to the job for you in your request. Pretty slick!

6. I suggest you use LinkedIn's Jobs Insider application. It will tell you all the people you and your friends are connected to when you are looking for jobs on other websites such as Monster, CareerBuilder, etc.

7. If you are being referred to someone in your job search whom you do not know, it is still best to contact them by phone or email instead of trying to connect with them directly in LinkedIn.

8. Under Contact Settings (LinkedIn.com/myprofile), make sure you include your email address and a phone number where a job poster can contact you

9. Also consider listing other emails, other than your primary one, that people might use to find you. You add these in Email Addresses under Personal Information on the Account & Settings tab.

10. Make sure you have enabled your profile to receive invites and direct contact (LinkedIn.com/secure/settings). See your Contact Settings page.

### 5 Tips for Your Job Search Using Facebook

Facebook was the second Social Media site I joined, and I like it. I have been using it more as a personal Social Networking site than a professional one, though. I think I started it that way to have another option. Plus, that was the way the site was originally positioned.

I suggest you take a different approach and consider using Facebook for business networking. If you've been using the site as a personal networking tool, you might need to change some of your privacy settings so you can transition your account while you're looking for a job.

*Tips for Facebook:*

1. Make sure you don't have any pictures posted that are not considered tasteful.

2. As with LinkedIn, make sure you have a professional-looking picture, not the one in your Speedo in Hawaii.

3. Similar to LinkedIn, Facebook allows you to post status updates. This capability is a great help because it provides a way for you to keep everyone up to date on your job search. It also serves as a subtle reminder to your Social Network that you are still seeking employment.

4. If you post a "Note" on Facebook, it will last longer than a status update. It also affords you more space to elaborate.

5. Consider creating a "Celebrity, Band, or Business Page." When you first go to www.facebook.com, you will see that selection at the bottom of the login section. Click on that option and then follow the outlined steps. Set yourself up as a celebrity. If you have trouble, call me and I will walk you through the process of setting up the page. That way, you can use your celebrity or business page for employers and not have to worry about co-mingling with your personal one.

### 5 Tips for Your Job Search Using Twitter

Twitter is the last Social Media profile I set up. The thing I really like about Twitter is that, believe it or not, you are limited on what you can say.

Initially a job search is like being a witness in court, which is precisely what I was doing the summer of 2008, long story. In any event, my lawyer George was always telling me less is better.

Like court, and my feelings on resumes, less can be better in the initial stages of the job search. I like Twitter because it is like a sound bite. People only have time for that little taste of information. Being confined to 140 characters really makes you think about what you're going to say. That's because you can't ramble on.

In the case of the job search, such a restriction is better. What you're doing with Twitter is giving people a little bit of a tease. So what are you going to tell them? You're going to hit them with your Unique Selling Proposition, of course. You're going to highlight what makes you better and different from all the other candidates.

With any bit of luck, your Twitter contacts will not feel as though they have enough information with that limited info. Then, hopefully, they will call you to talk further. NOW you have them engaging. You are becoming more of a real person to them. All of this increases the possibility of getting you some exposure.

One of the other main things I like about Twitter is that you can connect with people with whom you share a common interest, even if you do not know them personally. To me, that is the ultimate essence of networking.

*Twitter Tips:*

1. Connect with people you to not know but with whom you have something in common.

2. When you connect to someone on Twitter, the same rules apply as on all the other Social Networking sites. Make sure it makes sense for the reasons we discussed earlier.

3. Check out the job posting area.

4. Sign up for Twellow.com, which is like a Twitter yellow pages. There, you can look up the bios of everyone who has a Twitter account. Trust me when I say that this is one of the site's greatest and most helpful tools.

5. When you pick your Twitter name, if possible, select your real name to continue to brand yourself. If you have a middle name, use it. It will help you come up faster in the search engines.

### 8 Social Media Bonus Tips for Your Job Search

1. Create a blog. Be prepared to post to it frequently using your full name (including middle name/initial) and the main job title you are looking for. Experts tell you to post at least three times a week. The more often you post, however, the higher up your name will rank on the search engines when people are looking for you.

   Remember at all times to keep you blog professional and neutral regarding religion and political views. Keep in mind that whatever you post on the internet will stay there for years, so make sure you're proud of it.

   Look into:
   - www.wordpress.com
   - www.blogger.com
   - www.typepad.com
   
   For ideas on what to write about, go to:
   - www.blogsearch.google.com

2. Speaking of your name, don't forget to Google your name to see what prospective employers will find if they decide to do the same.

   This year, after hiring an employee (on their own without my help) and employing them for a full year, one of my clients did a Google search on that individual's name. The client found out that the employee was still working their other job at the same time they were working for my client. When they were offered the job, the new hire said they were giving up their job as a Realtor. Instead, they continued working as a Realtor and kept the associated real estate website up. As a result, my client felt as though the employee had not been truthful or kept their promise. In the end, the client hired my firm to find a replacement for the employee.

In addition to checking your name with Google, also go to www.zoominfo.com, www.naymz.com, and www.jigsaw.com and perform a self-search. Clarify any misinformation posted on those sites regarding yourself.

3. Look on www.Ning.com for industry connections and sites in your area. You may find some good contacts listed there.

4. Consider writing articles for your trade publications, local newspapers, trade associations, etc.

5. Brand yourself with your full name by buying the domain associated with it and setting up a simple website. Keep it simple.

As possible experts to help you with that idea, check out:
- www.GoDaddy.com
- www.1and1.com
- www.templatemonster.com

The important takeaway here is to remember that there are lots of ways you can use Social Media to power your job search. While it can be overwhelming at times, it's often worth the effort.

Start with the options you are the most comfortable with and then try a new one. Hang in there and endeavor to master the new technology before you move on to the next one.

There are some additional Social Media methods we did not touch on in this chapter, but I wanted to cover the ones that would have the most impact on your job search and which would be the easiest to learn and integrate into your job search.

Make it a goal today to pick one method you are currently not using in your job search and try it for 21 days. See the difference.

Good luck with your Social Media adventure this week. I invite you to contact me to share your feedback and adventures with me. Before I leave you, I close with this thought.

> *. . . that is what learning is. You suddenly*
> *understand something you've understood*
> *all your life, but in a new way.*
> —Doris Lessing

## Job Search Expert Action Plan

1 Take the reader Bonus Material, "Understanding the Power of Social Media" book list, to your local library to research the books listed.

2 Take out a book on LinkedIn, Facebook, and Twitter to study. See if you can stretch yourself and apply what you learn from these books.

3 Make sure you have a LinkedIn profile. Is should be complete and current.

4 Work on getting one recommendation a week from a past supervisor, peer, or vendor.

PART 4

# Job Search
# Success Answers

CHAPTER **12**

# Interview Questions
# That Change the Game

*Opportunity beckons more surely when
misfortune comes upon a person than
it ever does when that person is riding
the crest of a wave of success*

—EARL NIGHTINGALE

THE PRIMARY FOCUS of this chapter is to share with you some interview questions, strategies, and tips to improve your probability of being asked back for the second interview. The end goal of that second interview is, of course, to receive a job offer.

First, however, I would like to get into a brief preliminary conversation on getting ready for the interview process. Let's start with a general overview.

During the interview process, remember at all times to be yourself. You want to appear totally genuine and authentic to the hiring authority. People sense if you're putting on an act and will immediately be turned off. Make sure you speak with deep self- assuredness, humility, authority, wisdom, and a strong,

187

clear voice. You also want to make sure that your interviewers can clearly sense your confidence, enthusiasm, and ability so that they deem you a strong, decisive decision maker.

Needless to say, countless interview questions can be asked of you. In addition, there are countless resources available to you to research interview questions you may encounter. I have recently launched a blog to help supply additional information for you on this subject. You will find the blog address at the end this chapter as a resource you will want to use and share.

At all times, keep in mind that all the work you have done up to now in your job search process has helped you get to the point of being able to interview. Realize that you will get hired because of the quality with which you interview. How well you present yourself (build rapport) and your professional background, and how all that applies to the position you're interviewing for is the name of the game at this point.

Also bear in mind that the people who are ultimately hired are not always the best at doing the job. ***Rather, they are the best at getting the job.*** People hire people they like. Hence, they will often go for the person who might be more personable on the job. So remember to be yourself and to speak enthusiastically. Make sure the interviewer has a sense of not only who you are as a person but also your personality.

People will hire someone they know, like, and trust. You need to focus on communicating and building a relationship with the interviewer, to the point that by the end of the interview they feel they know you, like you, and trust that you can do the job.

### Interview—What to Expect

During the first interview, the interviewer should speak at least 60% of the time. In subsequent interviews, that percentage decreases, with you doing more of the talking.

Let's set the stage for the interview process. Following are the three primary stages you'll likely encounter while interviewing:

1. The rapport-building process starts the minute you meet the interviewer. It involves the dialogue you exchange (primarily the small talk you engage in during the initial introductions).

2. The information-exchange process takes place when you uncover the hiring authority's needs and connect with them on those main points. This stage takes place during the bulk of the actual interviewing portion.

    Here is where you hope to discover the possibilities that exist at the company in which you can make a difference. Once you have done so, you then need to articulate a valid connection where your background will help the organization.

3. The summary and closing portions of the interview process are where you briefly summarize the main points of the interview and acknowledge your interest in and appreciation for the opportunity to interview.

    You also acknowledge that there is a mutual fit. If you are not sure how you feel about the position at this time, keep that opinion to yourself. You may change your mind with additional information and future interviews. The main thing is you want to keep your options open. The more the hiring authority gets to know you as a person, the more they will be willing to modify the position in the areas where you have realistic concerns. If the job is a total mismatch and you are willing to walk away from the company forever, and then tell the interviewer politely that you are not interested at this time.

    Ask if there are any objections or concerns about your background relative to you being seriously considered as a candidate for the position. Handle all of the hiring authority's objections at this time. The more time that lingers with a negative feeling about your background or a misunderstanding of your answers being harbored, the harder it is to turn the situation around. **The sooner you address any negative concerns or misunderstandings the better it is for you!**

Ask what the next step is. The answer to this question will give you a sense of the hiring authority's timing. At this time, you can even ask them if there is a suggested time period at which you should follow up with them regarding the next step.

One of the BIGGEST MYTHS with the hiring process is that the interviewer's sense of urgency to fill the position is the same as yours. *In actuality, their sense of urgency to fill the position is usually slower than yours. Patience is the key here.*

Two styles of interviewing typically exist:

1. **Traditional job interviews** that tend to use broad-based questions (commonly felt to be 10% predictive of future on-the-job-behavior)
   a. Does the job seeker have the needed skills?
   b. Does the job seeker have the ability to do the job?
   c. Does the job seeker have the desired enthusiasm?
   d. Does the job seeker have the work ethics the employer expects?
   e. Will the job seeker be a team player and fit into the organization?

2. **Behavioral job interviews** that tend to look at past experience as an indicator of future behavior by using specific questions (commonly felt to be 55% predictive of future on-the-job behavior)
   Such interviews use questions that look into past specific behaviors. (SAR+1) (SAR = Situation → Action Taken → Results Achieved
   They usually entail these types of questions:
   a. Describe a situation/problem that applies to the question.
   b. Discuss what type of action you took for the situation.

c. Give the details of the result/outcome.

d. Share what you learned from that situation.

Have a list of six to seven examples from your past experience. Apply the above four questions to them and practice them before your interview. I suggest you type up your answers to make everything clear and succinct in your mind.

In coming up with this list, use three accomplishments from your resume and three negative situations you either turned around or made the best of the outcome. Try to pick negative situation examples that are earlier in your career, further back in time.

During the interview process, remember at all times to appear fully authentic and genuine.

### Let's Look at 10 Types of Interviews

When interviewing with a company, you will most often find yourself in the following situations.

1. Unstructured Interview
   - More open-ended questions

2. Structured Interview
   - You are asked questions from a list.

3. Informational Interview
   - Where you network for information, not a job

4. Screening Interview
   - Phone interview (majority)
   - Face-to-face interview (more for local candidates)

5. One-on-One Interviews (most common of all)
   - Individual interview

6. Group Interviews
   - Committee interview

- Joint interview (two to three candidates interviewed at the same time)
- Department interview

7. Interactive Interviews
    - Professional portfolio interview
    - Shadow interview (where you spend time "on the job")
    - Case interview (where you are asked to provide a solution to an actual problem)

8. Multimedia Interviews
    - Computerized interviews (where you answer questions on a computer for one to two hours)
    - Videoconferencing interview (50% of Fortune 500 companies use this type of interview.)

9. Lunch Interview

10. Stress Interview (The key is to remain calm under pressure.)

Lately, in the new economy, it seems as though the majority of first interviews are being conducted via phone. This change has evolved because of the time efficiency of the telephone interview as well as the vast number of candidates the hiring authority has available to screen from. The phone interview has become the first interview of choice by the majority of hiring authorities, because it helps them quickly cull a long list of candidates. It saves them both time and money!

### 12 Professional Secrets to a Successful Phone Interview

1. *Remember that the purpose of a phone interview is to get the face-to-face interview.*

2. Make sure you have a professional, outgoing greeting on your phone for the times you are unavailable to answer.

3. Use a land line for the phone interview as opposed to a cell phone.

4. Make sure you are in a quiet location, far from distractions.

5. If possible, be the one who places the call so you can have control over exactly when the interview takes place.

6. Make sure the time that is set up is specific rather than a large time span.

7. Make sure you allow enough time away from other commitments for the call. A rule of thumb is to allow an hour. Most phone interviews take less time than that.

8. Dress for the session. Studies have shown that you will project yourself in a more confident and professional manner if you are dressed in business attire.

9. Standing up during the phone interview will help improve the strength of your voice and your answers. That is because you will be speaking from your diaphragm. As a result, your voice will be energized.

10. Speak clearly and enunciate.

11. Let the interviewer hang up the phone and end the conversation first. Following this simple yet gracious social gesture leaves the other party with a subtly biased good feeling toward you.

12. Don't forget to follow up with a thank-you note within 24 hours.

### 3 Questions They Will Ask

What are the top three interview questions that are asked in some way by most interviewers?

1. *Do you have the qualifications? Can you do the job?*

With this question the interviewer is evaluating whether you have the technical background, training, education, capabilities, and experience to perform the job.

- Do you have a valid track record of results and accomplishments that match the position you're interviewing for?
- Do you have the knowledge, intelligence, and political savvy to get the job done?

2. *Will you fit in with our organization?*
   - Does the hiring authority envision you interacting with their team?
   - Do you have a personality that shows a level of flexibility and a management style that can accommodate changes?
   - Are you a team player?
   - How well will you get along with your future boss and peers?
   - How well will you get along with your subordinate staff?

   The person hiring you is asking themselves, "If I make the decision to hire this individual, will that decision reflect well or poorly on me within the organization? Ideally, they want to see you as a good fit for their organization in terms of core values, personality, the ability to work with others, and the suitability to be part of their team.

3. *Why do you want the job?*
   I cannot stress enough how much of a difference strong enthusiasm plays in the interviewing process.
   - Did you appear to the hiring authority as though you came fully prepared for the interview?
   - Did you do your homework in advance?
   - How much research on the company did you do in advance?

- How much did you engage and actively participate in the interviewing process and with all those with whom you interviewed?

### 4 Answers Employers are Looking For

1. Why specifically is this person interested in working for our company?

2. What problems will this person be able to solve for us? Does this person have the skill level and expertise we are looking for in this job?

3. Why should I hire this person above all the other candidates? What makes this individual the best?

4. What compensation is this person looking for relative to what I'm able to pay?

Remember that during the entire process, the interviewer is evaluating your answers relative to these four questions plus the previous three. Make sure you know what your answers to all of these questions will be during the interview. Practice aloud your written answers to all of the questions I am sharing with you, in preparation for your interviews.

### How to Handle 21 of the More Challenging Interview Scenarios

1. The unanticipated question from leftfield
      If during the interviewing process you find that you are asked a question you had not anticipated that slightly throws you off, here is a technique to help you handle the situation. This same strategy can be used when you are asked a particularly difficult question. The important thing is to remain confident at all times.
      The approach I suggest will help you buy a little time during the interviewing process. It will allow you to think

on your feet. At the same time, it will not diminish your self-confidence.

My suggested response to the awkward or sometimes unanticipated broad or particularly difficult question is, "I'm sorry but I have never been asked that question before. While I'd like to think more about that question, what comes immediately to my mind is the following situation . . ." And then you proceed to elaborate.

2. The pregnant pause . . . intended

If you sense that someone may be using this technique on you to unnerve you, then in a helpful tone counter, "Is there anything else you'd like to know about . . . (the question you just finished answering)? Treat it as a lapse of attention on the interviewer's part. That is the only way to deal with it.

3. *What salary are you looking for?*

You do not answer this question with a salary figure. You merely say, "While I appreciate that you're asking me that question, I feel as though it may be a bit premature. Right now I'm more interested in getting additional information about your company and the position. I'm sure you know what the fair market value is for someone with my type of experience. You strike me as a fair type of guy/gal. In the event that an offer was to be extended to me, I would expect nothing but a fair one. If it is all right with you, I would like to get back to discussing the position."

4. Anxiety over being considered overqualified

During the interview, make sure that you express interest, admiration, and enthusiasm for both the position and the company. Nothing wins over a hiring manager more than a positive attitude and a passion for the job and the employer.

If you are sensing that the interviewer may be deeming you overqualified, you can address the issue head on. Simply ask, "What can I do to convince you that I'm the best candidate for the job?"

5. *Tell me about yourself.*

This is a great open-ended line of questioning, but you have to be careful not to wander off. Don't ramble on and on about information that the interviewer is not really looking for or does not really care about. Keep it brief. You can even ask them if there is a specific time period or part of your resume they are particularly interested in.

Also, use my interview questions sheet in the reader Bonus Material for this chapter. The following question is on that sheet, which is titled "Sweet Questions."

When asked to talk about yourself, you say, "It would help me to answer that question if you could give me an idea of what the three most important traits or characteristics are that you're looking for in an ideal job candidate." Then sit back, wait, and listen. If you are able to pose this question of the interviewer, use their answer to guide your response. You then take three mini success stories or SAR situations that are appropriate to the situation and share that information with them. That way, you are really giving them the relevant answers they are looking for. In essence, you are addressing their "hot buttons."

6. *Describe to me a project you were involved with where you were disappointed in your own performance.*

Use your answer to describe to the interviewer what you learned from that experience. Show how your skills have helped you to overcome barriers you've encountered in the past and how you learned from those experiences.

7. *What is the most difficult work or personal experience you've ever had to face?*

Here, the interviewer is looking to find out how you operate under pressure. Provide an example of a problem that had you under an unusual amount of pressure and how you resolved the situation. What was the end result?

8. *Tell me how you have handled criticism of your work in the past.*

The interviewer is trying to see if you have a sense of accepting responsibility for your actions. This question gives them insight into your professional character.

Tell them about a situation where you faced a problem and overcame it. You want to conclude your response by discussing what you learned from the experience. You never want to talk negatively about any past associates or organizations.

9. *Which aspects of your work are criticized most often?*

Ideally, your answer should give an example of something you overlooked or a mistake you made early on in your career. Respond with something like, "As a result of that learning experience, I pay more careful attention to that type of detail in all my work."

10. *Which work habit would your current/recent boss like to see you change the most?*

One way to approach this question is to explain a minor difference or preference between you and your past supervisor. Alternatively, explain a weakness you and your boss have worked on together to improve. It is important to show that the habit is a minor weakness that you recognized early and worked hard on to fix. The further back in your professional career this habit goes, the better an example it is.

11. *Describe a situation at work that frustrated you.*

This is a line of questioning where the interviewer is trying to gain insight into your professional personality. They are looking for an example where you were able to handle a difficult situation without being offensive, non-professional, or closed-minded. Provide an example that shows you are able to work through problems with tact and without creating hard feelings.

12. *Tell me about a failed project, a project that did not work out.*

Describe how you learned from the situation. Go on to explain how the situation has changed your professional and leadership style. Tell the interviewer, in hindsight, what you should have and could have done instead.

13. *Tell me about your least favorite past supervisor.*

The interviewer is testing you on how you will speak of your previous superiors. Do not fall into the trap of talking negatively about anyone with whom you have worked in the past. If forced to discuss a situation, pick one that is not too negative, be brief, and focus on what you learned from the experience.

14. *Who is the toughest boss you ever had to work for and why?*

Here again, you are being set up to talk negatively of someone. Instead, share an example of a situation where this boss taught you something new. Divulge to the interviewer the positive traits this boss possessed in addition to the qualities that made him or her tough.

15. *Share with me an example when you had a real problem getting along with one of your business associates.*

Try to think of an example involving a difference in work ethics. You do not want to share an example regarding personality clashes. In choosing an example, communicate how you solved the problem and share the results.

16. *Have you ever had to work for a manager who was difficult to get along with or whom you thought was unfair to you?*

   Again, you need to avoid any negative comments about any individuals. The interviewer is testing you to see if you're the type to badmouth people.

17. *Share with me an example on how you handled tension with your boss.*

   Answer this question in the past tense. Discuss a boss you had earlier in your career. Try to think of an example involving miscommunication. Then focus on how the two of you worked through that situation. Explain the steps you have taken to make sure that situation has not arisen again.

18. *What would you say if I told you that you were not doing a good job interviewing today?*

   This is a classic example of a stress question. You need to stay calm and relaxed. Do not let your confidence be shaken.

   You could start off by asking the interviewer to share with you the specific parts of the interviewing process where perhaps you have not fully or properly communicated. Then tell them that you would like to review those areas and questions again to clarify more fully or appropriately the areas that were misunderstood.

19. *Sell me this pen, stapler, etc.*

   The interviewer is testing to see how quickly you can think on your feet. You should be prepared to give a 30-second sales pitch on the benefits, features, and advantages of the suggested product.

20. *Describe to me an example where you applied a time management skill that you learned to a work situation.*

The interviewer is looking for an example where you worked to make your work environment a more productive one. If possible, explain how you helped increase productivity and save money.

21. *Prove to me that your interest in this job and company is sincere and genuine.*

You need to demonstrate a strong interest in the organization and the position. Use the information from your research to talk about the specific position and the company details that make you want to become an employee.

### Tips to Overcoming Stereotypes

1. "Too young, not enough experience"

Respond to this insinuation by discussing your early career experience that may not be on your resume. Also mention any civic, non-profit volunteer positions you have held that may help demonstrate additional experience that is not on your resume.

2. Age (too old)

Make sure the interviewer sees you as a high-energy person who maintains a vigorous physical-activity level and keeps a fast-paced schedule.

Last year, I placed an individual, David, who was 65 years old as a National Sales Manager for a client of mine. David looked like he was in his late 50s with a very high professional image, a nice way of dressing, and a good physique. Apparently, the only medicine he takes is an occasional aspirin when he gets sore. Throughout the entire job search process, he also portrayed himself as a high-energy person. In particular, he highlighted his strong computer skills throughout the interviewing process. I did not find out he was 65 until after I extended my client's offer to him. That is when he told me he did not need the medical coverage because of his age! (He was covered by Medicare.)

3. Gender (for women)

    If you're a woman, make sure the interviewer knows that you are accustomed to extensive travel and making difficult decisions and that you can operate independently. During the interview process, also try adding an anecdote that makes it clear your household is organized and can run without you.

4. Overweight

    Stress the fact that you lead a highly disciplined and energetic life. Accentuate that you work toward long-term goals and that you adhere to demanding self-imposed schedules.

More creative, unusual questions you could be asked during a job interview include:

1. If you were a box of cereal, what type of cereal would you be and why?

2. If you were a car, what type of car would you be and why?

3. If you were a frog in a tree, what would you be doing?

4. What is your favorite holiday and why?

5. If you were a season, which one would you be and why?

As part of the Bonus Material at the end of this chapter, I review with you a set of questions I have shared with all my job candidates over the years. These powerful questions can be posed of the interviewer to evoke answers that will supply important information about the position you are interviewing for and want!

In closing, remember what I said at the beginning: Be yourself. Be sincere, genuine, and truthful and you will be that much closer to receiving a job offer.

Present yourself as a top-shelf professional executive who comes across as enthusiastic and confident. The first two minutes are the most important. You need to establish a good rapport with the interviewer that will carry on consistently throughout the entire interview.

Also, remember to take your lists of questions with you. Depending on the amount of time the interviewer has allotted for the interview, you may not be able to ask all of them. You will have to gauge yourself there.

I suggest that, in addition to the questions I have shared with you here, you find more. Please look on my blog, www.GreatInterviewQuestionsBlog.com, and go to your local library to take out several books on interview questions. Read through the additional interview questions you find, and practice your answers aloud, with a friend if possible. Remember to keep your answers succinct! Above all else, speak clearly with a confident voice!

*Success has a price tag on it, and the tag reads,*
*COURAGE, DETERMINATION, DISCIPLINE, RISK*
*TAKING, PERSEVERANCE, AND CONSISTENCY—*
*doing the RIGHT THING for the RIGHT REASONS*
*and not just when we feel like it.*
—James M. Meston

## Bonus Material
Following are the four primary questions you should ask the interviewer at the end of your interview:

1. *What three traits or characteristics are you looking for in the ideal candidate for this position?*
   a. Three helps people get specific and narrows in on the most important traits.

b. This line of questioning enables the interviewer to follow up their answer with mini success stories that specifically address their top three needs.

2. *What problems do you currently have in the department (e.g., marketing /sales) that are not being resolved that you would like to see resolved in the next six months, one year, three years?*
    This question will give you a perspective on whether or not the hiring authority's goals are realistic.

3. *Is there anything about me or my background that causes you some concern in terms of me being seriously considered for this position?*
    Handle all objections on the spot.

4. *What is the next step from here?*
    Get a sense of the interviewer's timing.

## Job Search Expert Action Plan

1 Visit my blog at www.GreatInterview QuestionsBlog.com for my great interview questions and suggested answers. They will help strengthen your interview.

2 Study and review your reader Bonus Material, "Sweet Questions—Powerful Interview Questions."

3 Write out your answers to some of these questions.

4 Practice your answers and questions aloud with a friend, loved one, or support person.

If you are feeling brave, record or videotape your answers to these questions. After you have listened to your recording (and recovered), rework your weak answers to make them more succinct and stronger.

CHAPTER **13**

# Negotiate the Salary
# You Want and Deserve
# in This Current Market

*When we do more than we are paid to do,*
*eventually we will be paid more for what we do.*

—ZIG ZIGLAR

IN THIS NEW ECONOMY, the competition is tough and the line of equally qualified candidates is long. Chances are, you're finding yourself vying for the same job dozens of others are. You need to keep these tendencies in mind when considering a job offer.

### Overall Negotiation Strategy

There are three key points to salary negotiation that you must focus on. They are:

1. Know what your current fair-market-value compensation is.

2. Know clearly which of your strengths and accomplishments you intend to consistently communicate and leverage throughout the interviewing process.

3. Delay any salary conversations as long as possible.

## Salary Negotiations Started Yesterday

The salary negotiations start the minute you apply for a job. In the case of networking, they begin as soon as you call the contact you have been referred to by one of your leads.

That being said, it behooves you to do your research before your first phone or face-to-face interview. Prior to applying for any positions or contacting any leads, you need to research the company, the position title, the industry, and the geographic location. This myriad of variables will affect what is considered fair market value for the position you are thinking of applying for.

You owe it to both yourself and your family to invest the extra time on the front end doing serious research. That way you can determine the realistic salary for your level of responsibility. This salary range will vary by job occupation, employment level, industry, geography (cost of living), and, at times, the size of the organization itself.

Smaller companies will sometimes pay above fair market rate to attract the caliber of talent they are looking for. It's their way of competing with their industry's "big guys."

Note also that companies in less desirable geographical locations will sometimes also pay higher wages than fair market value. By doing so, they can attract the caliber of talent they're looking for.

After you have done all your research, you should then have a sense of a realistic salary range you should be seeking relative to your professional background. This is the pay range you want to keep in the forefront of your mind during your salary negotiations.

## Special Resources to Assist You in Your Salary Research

Following is a list of some websites you should use as a starting point in your salary research. This information will confirm your fair market value for each position you are interviewing for.

Remember that you will need to do this research for every title you are considering. Hypothetically, each job title could have a different salary range within the same geographic location. This is particularly true when evaluating different geographic locations for each job title.

When coming up with a salary figure, try the following sources for information:

1.  Compare your past salary history to the current suggested compensation for the title/position.

2.  Leverage industry trade associations and industry contacts to reconfirm fair market compensation within your industry or new industries you are considering entering.

3.  Network with anybody you know internally in any of the companies you are interviewing with. Contact them to see if they can offer you any assistance on compensation information relative to the positions you are interviewing for. They will be able to give you an indication of whether the company pays fair market value or is light on its salary offers.

In the Bonus Material for this chapter, I will be including several salary-related websites, government websites, and reference books you can turn to for more assistance in devising a fair compensation scheme.

### Real-World Examples
Overall, the main goal of all your research is to gain insight into the realistic salary range for the type of position you are interested in and, hopefully, interviewing for. Coming up with a general dollar figure, however, is just the tip of the iceberg.

Remember that you should also research the company itself. You may be able to uncover the salary range of the actual position you're vying for or the position either below or above it.

The combination of these ideas should give you a solid salary range to work with. You can uncover this information on the company's corporate website, on one of the major job posting sites, or by networking with current and past employees. If all else fails, you also can contact the firm's competitors and see if you are able to uncover their salary ranges, which should be similar.

The key to salary negotiation is to understand what the position's compensation range is. You are just trying to figure out the company's benchmarks and where within that salary span the hiring authority will realistically give you an offer. Then of course, you have to decide whether that offer is a fair one you would seriously consider.

### Setting Your Value from the Start

Know clearly which of your strengths and accomplishments you intend to consistently communicate throughout the interviewing process. Ideally, this showcasing should start with your initial communication in the form of your customized cover letter and resume.

The more the prospective employer understands the value and benefit you bring to the organization, the closer the compensation negotiations will approach the salary you desire and deserve.

Make sure this information is clearly communicated during the entire interview process. The hiring authority needs to understand the type of impact and contributions you're going to be able to make to both the individual department and the company as a whole. Communicate your **value** clearly to them. Make sure they understand how you will make money for them, save them money, and solve their problems for them!

You want to make sure the hiring authority understands your value equation (i.e., the sum total of everything you bring to the table). Collectively, all of this will hopefully translate into a fair offer.

The more responsibility you can assume for your potential employer, the higher the compensation you will be offered. It's as simple as that. This is why it's important you are communicating to the hiring authority what you are capable of accomplishing for them throughout the entire process. They must clearly understand what you have to offer. Otherwise, you will end up with an offer that is lighter than it should be.

If the prospective employer understands the value you bring to their organization, then they will be convinced that you can do the job. As a result, they will be compelled to make you a fair offer.

If, on the other hand, they do not understand your background and how it fits their needs, you may receive an offer that is lower than what you desire. Keep in mind that it will be much harder to negotiate uphill at the end than it will be from the outset. That said you want to sell them on your strengths and accomplishments as soon as possible, rather than waiting until the salary negotiation at the end.

## What to Do When the Salary Is Lower Than What You're Seeking

If you find that a position you are interested in is too light in the salary department relative to your professional background and expertise but it's reasonably close, continue on with the interviewing process.

Yes, I suggest you go forward with the interview anyway, but with an ulterior motive in mind. During the end of the first interview, I would then suggest you bring up the possibility of adding additional duties or responsibilities that will warrant a higher pay scale. Make sure these add-ons will make the job more interesting to you and that both you and the hiring authority agree on them. In addition, remember to confirm these details in your follow-up letters.

This is a technique I have used in just about every search I've worked on. I like to up the job description ante so that the position is customized for both the candidate and the employer.

In the case of working through a recruiter who does not use or understand this technique, you will need to be the one who handles the job-responsibility negotiations yourself. There's nothing shady about this technique. In fact, by employing it, you'll creatively outmaneuver the other candidates for the position. In the end, they will end up being under-qualified for the upgraded final position, which you had a hand in redesigning.

Once you've added on responsibilities, throughout the remainder of the interviews continue to confirm that the hiring authority still agrees with them. Also, remind them in your follow-up letters that you will satisfy all the needs for the position. Be sure to offer to answer any concerns the hiring authority may have about you or your background relative to the position you are being considered for.

The goal here is to chip away at the possibility of increasing your responsibility or authority above and beyond the original job description. On the basis of these added duties, the job has now, in essence, changed. In turn, the salary should change as well. Now you've opened the door to possible upward salary negotiations. Congratulations!

### Delay—You Never Want to Lead with a Number

You want to delay any salary conversations for as long as possible. To that end, do not bring up salary before the employer does. Try to delay the compensation conversation at least until you know exactly what the position entails.

Remember at all times to avoid any questions regarding salary that would cause you to lead a negotiation and basically end up negotiating with yourself. This type of situation always puts you in a weaker position.

### You Never Want to Lead with a Salary Number!

Information is power in all negotiations. This is particularly true when looking for a job. Your goal with your job search should be to always hold on to your power as long as possible.

The longer you delay the salary talk, the more you situate yourself to negotiate from the best possible position, which is ideally after the employer has offered you the job. At that point, but before you accept, is your greatest point of leverage in the salary negotiation process.

If you are working with a recruiter, this part of the process will be much easier for you. That's because traditionally, all salary questions are handled by the recruiter on your behalf.

### Reality of the Salary History Issue

The reality is that most employers will ask you to supply a salary history to them when you submit your cover letter and resume or when they send you a job application.

Salary requirements can be included in your cover letter with a sentence such as: "My salary requirements are negotiable based upon the job responsibilities and the total compensation package."

The key is to dance around such requests but not ignore them. If you do not supply the requested salary history, you will most likely be labeled as difficult and/or screened out.

When supplying your salary history, always tell the truth. You can try the approach of applying a compensation range to the salary history for your most recent or current position if it included a bonus.

For example, "My salary requirements is in the $XX,XXX+ range. I am very interested in your organization/company and I know we can work something out."

Given how competitive the market currently is, you do want to be careful, however, and not "blow yourself out of the ballpark." It is definitely a buyer's (employer's) market right now in this new economy.

### Answers for "What Salary Are You Looking For?"

*Following are several compensation-related questions you may encounter during the interview process along with my recommended responses. Use these suggested answers as a template.*

QUESTION: What salary are you currently looking for?
ANSWER: "I appreciate that you are asking me that question, but I must say, (interviewer's first name), I consider it a bit

premature at this point. At the moment, I'm really more interested in talking to you about the position and the organization, (if that is all right with you). Also, (interviewer's name), I'm sure you're aware of the fair market value for someone with my type of professional background. You strike me as a fair type of person, and in the event that an offer was extended to me, I would expect it to be nothing but a fair one. (Now if it's all right with you), I'd really like to get back to our conversation regarding the position and your company."

QUESTION: What salary are you currently looking for?

ANSWER: "I'm much more interested in doing (the type of work you're interviewing for) here at (the name of the company) than I am in the size of the *initial* offer."

As a job search expert, I have found that 40% of the time this line of reasoning will take care of the situation. Realize at this point that you have clearly differentiated yourself from the majority of candidates by focusing on the job rather than the compensation. If the interviewer comes back and repeats the question, try this alternate response.

ANSWER: "I will *consider any reasonable* offer."

I like this approach because the words "consider any reasonable" are very broad-based. Such an open-ended response keeps the door open to your advantage. At the same time, it makes you come across as being polite.

If the interviewer still comes back and repeats the question a third time (and this will happen only approximately 30% of the time), then turn the tables.

ANSWER: "(Interviewer's first name), you are in a much better position to know how much I'm worth to you than I am. Again, you strike me as a fair type of person, and I would expect nothing but a fair offer from you."

QUESTION: What salary are you looking for? What are you salary requirements?

ANSWER: "What is the range you normally pay for this position, or what do you consider this position to be worth?"

Or

ANSWER: "My requirements are flexible" or "My salary is negotiable."

The aim is to put off the salary discussion as long as possible—ideally until you get an actual job offer.

### How the Offer is Determined

When extending you a job offer, the company will take into account the following in coming up with a compensation dollar figure.

1. Your work experience, career path, professional area of job expertise, and the fair market salary for similar people with the same type of background in the same industry will affect the salary offer.

2. Typical salaries found in the employer's industry can impact their salary structure, with salaries varying from industry to industry.

3. The size of the company can affect the salary offered. (As previously mentioned, smaller companies tend to pay more to attract the best talent and to compete with larger companies.) Companies in remote locations traditionally have trouble recruiting talent to their locations. As a result, they tend to offer compensation above fair market value to attract the talent they need.

4. The geographic location and cost of living will affect the salary offer.

5. Current demand for and availability of job seekers with a similar professional background to yours will have an impact on the salary offered.

   For example, if there is a shortage of electrical engineers (EE) in a certain geographic location, then the compensation offered to fill a void in the marketplace may be higher than fair market value for that same position prior to the shortage. It's a classic supply and demand issue.

6. The amount of money that has been budgeted for the position will bear weight on the salary being offered.

Please note that in this new economy, some of the compensations have gone down (decreased), in a manner similar to the stock market and housing market. In addition, the excess number of job seekers currently in the market has driven down some of the compensations.

### Will You Accept the Offer?

Before you flat-out accept or reject a salary offer, you need to do some mental calculation. Compute what the *total* compensation is. The actual offer will be extended in terms of not only base salary but also other components such as bonus, company car, medical coverage, etc.

Also, always make sure you get your offer in writing once you have negotiated a final compensation you consider reasonable.

You need to factor in three variables when deciding whether or not to accept a salary offer.

1. The current realistic market value for someone with your type of experience

2. The value the company places on someone with your type of professional background

3. What the job is worth to you

All three of these components will have an impact on whether the offer is fair or good in your mind.

### You Have an Offer! "Congratulations!" Now What?

Congratulations! Now what?

1. Thank the person for the offer. Be polite, enthusiastic, and gracious, even if you are disappointed in the offer.

2. Traditionally you will be given anywhere between 24 hours and a week to consider the offer. My suggestion is not to accept on the spot but to tell the hiring authority that you would like some time to consider the offer fully. Ask them when they would like you to get back to them.

If you know you are happy with the offer, including salary, realistic bonus, vacation time, etc., then tell the hiring authority you will give them a call in 24 hours. If you are disappointed in the offer, now is when you want to see if you can buy yourself a little time to consider negotiating the offer more to your liking, assuming you have realistic expectations. (If you are working through a recruiter, they will be assisting you with this entire process.)

A fair number of people make the mistake of thinking about the salary offer in terms of what they feel they need or deserve rather than what their value is. This goes back to the beginning of this chapter.

- What is your fair market value? (This is where your salary research information, taking into account title, experience, industry, geographical location, and current market conditions, comes into play.)
- What is your value to the prospective employer? Do they appreciate and understand your accomplishments, strengths, and achievements? Do they understand the extra value you bring to the position and the organization?
- What are the organizational needs and challenges you can solve?
- Did you effectively communicate the type of impact you can expect to make, the problems you will solve, and the revenue you will generate?

If you feel you may have fallen short in any of these areas during the interviewing process, then subtly communicate this information when you attempt to negotiate a higher offer.

In today's market it will not be as easy to negotiate as it was when there was a shortage of strong talent. Bear in mind that the employer is currently in the driver's seat. Don't try to take the wheel, only to find yourself out of contention.

3. Be prepared to negotiate in areas other than base salary, such as:
   a. Sign-on bonus to bridge a base salary that was lower than desired
   b. Higher performance bonus
   c. Company car where one usually does not exist or a higher car allowance
   d. More vacation time
   e. A shorter timeframe for a performance review and raise (three, six, or nine months)

Now is the time to be creative!

4. Do not negotiate the situation to the point of alienating the hiring authority. All negotiations should be treated as a win-win. Always use a conversational tone and avoid being confrontational.

Once your future employer has agreed to your compensation requests, the negotiations are over. At this time, ask for a revised letter with the new offer outlined and accept! Most companies will put their offer in writing. If they do not, repeat the offer in your acceptance letter to make sure everyone is on the same page.

Understand that you may not always be able to negotiate the job offer. I would suggest that given the current economy, this tendency may hold true more often than ever.

Go into your business mind and heart and decide if this job makes sense, both career-wise and financially. You may have to accept something that is not perfect but at least keeps you in the game.

My suggestion is to try to stay with any job you accept for at least a year before leaving. Give it a fair shake. Things may be better, more challenging, and interesting than you originally understood during the interview.

> *Do a little more than you're paid to;*
> *Give a little more than you have to;*
> *Try a little harder than you want to;*
> *Aim a little higher than you think possible;*
> *And give a lot of thanks to God for*
> *health, family, and friends.*
> —Art Linkletter

## 12 Salary Bonus Resources

### 7 Salary Websites

Following are some websites that will help you with your salary compensation research.

1. www.jobstar.org—one of the earliest websites on the internet to share salary information. Go specifically to: www.jobstar.org/tools/salary/index.cfm.

2. www.Jobnob.com—a good tool for job seekers in search of salary information. Here, you can find actual salary information (as opposed to the industry averages you receive at other salary sites) according to job title or company. You can also then browse jobs (by company or profession). Data is employer-reported. There is no cost to the job seekers using this service.

3. www.JobSearchIntelligence.com—a great salary research tool for job seekers, with a comprehensive set of questions to provide accurate compensation data. Currently

offers information on 480 occupations, within 560 geographic regions. Sources include the U.S. Department of Labor, the U.S. Bureau of Labor Statistics, the U.S. Census Bureau, the U.S. Equal Employment Opportunity Commission, the U.S. Bureau of Economic Analysis, and previous job seekers. There is no cost to job seekers using this service.

4. www.PayScale.com—a salary assessment site that matches job seekers' job profiles with expected compensation via comparisons to compensation packages of job seekers with similar skills and experiences, rather than simple job titles or zip code comparisons. The basic report is free, while more detailed reports are fee-based.

5. www.Salary.com—If you're looking for help in determining the value of a job offer or what you are worth on the job market, then you should visit this site. Here, a large collection of salary reports on virtually every occupation have been compiled. Free, but you'll have to work around the ads.

6. www.SalaryExpert.com—a large salary site offering salaries, benefits, and cost-of-living information for 30,000 positions in more than 45,000 locations. Job seekers can find accurate salary data here. The site even shows its sources for the information. From Baker, Thomsen Associates Insurance Services, Inc., this site is free for job seekers.

7. www.SalaryList.com—provides real person, real position, real job, and associated real salary information for many U.S. job titles, by job, company, and state. The site is maintained by MacroKey Data Research Group. There is no cost to the job seeker. (I find this site to be a particularly good one.)

Suggested Government Websites

As a cross-reference to the sites listed above, I suggest you visit the following government websites:

1. For salaries by occupation, the Bureau of Labor Statistics: www.bls.gov/oco—This takes you into *The Occupational Outlook Handbook 2010–2011,* where you will find a wealth of useful information.

2. For salaries by industry, the Bureau of Labor Statistics: www.stats.bls.gov/oes/oes_emp.htm—This takes you to the "Occupational Employment Statistics" report, where you will find 26+ industries listed along with their salary information.

*Reference Books to Look for at the Library*

1. *The New Guide to Occupational Exploration*

2. *Occupational Outlook Handbook*

3. *O\*NET Directory of Occupational Titles*

---

## Job Search Expert Action Plan

1 Go to the seven salary websites I suggest in this chapter.

2 Create an Excel spreadsheet where you can track your favorite salary website and different job titles. This will help you when you go to average the different salary information from the various sites. It will give you a sense of what is currently a "realistic" salary for the positions you are researching.

3 Go to the big job boards and see if you are able to uncover salary ranges for similar industry job titles.

4    Match the salary website numbers against the big job boards.

5    Take the two sources and recalculate your average again.

6    This research should be done again after your second interview with a company in anticipation of a possible offer. It will ensure you have "current" salary market information going into a salary negotiation.

7    In this new economy remember to be realistic. A bird in the hand is worth two in the bush.

8    The new economy reality is that salary compensations have come down right along with the housing market and stock market.

# CHAPTER 14

# Secrets of the Job Search for the Over 45 Crowd

*Our society automatically scraps people just like old automobiles. It's the Detroit syndrome, but the latest models are not always the best.*

—MARGARET KUHN

THOSE OF YOU WHO ARE over 45 may encounter a special challenge associated with the job search process: being prejudged unfairly prior to your second interview or, in some cases, first interview. Combating this tendency means creating a favorable presentation environment both on paper and in person. The goal here is to ideally be judged on the strengths and talents you bring to the prospective organization rather than being screened out "prematurely" as a result of your "maturity."

According to November 2010 data from the Bureau of Labor Statistics, displaced workers who are age 55 and older will tend to be out of work 35 weeks, which is 20% longer than job seekers who are between 25 and 54 years of age.

*In This Current Job Market*

- You will be lucky if its recipient spends more than 15 seconds reading your paperwork.
- It takes 100 to 200 resumes to land a job.
- It will take 15 to 20 phone calls to get one interview.
- 1 out of 12 informational interviews will land a job.
- It takes approximately 30 interviews to land a job (3–5 months).
- 80% of jobs are found in the "Hidden Job Market." That means they will never be posted.
- 85% of job seekers are landing their jobs through networking.
- The first four to five minute of the interview is the most critical timeframe. It's very hard to reverse a bad first impression. An unfavorable initial impression is seldom changed later on.
- Some say that the first minute of the interview is actually the most critical of all.

### How to Improve 93% of Your First Impression

According to Professor Albert Mehrabian (UCLA), there are three different elements that affect our first impression when we meet with someone. These elements affect whether we make a positive first impression or not. Relative to your first impression, your:

- Words impact 7% of your overall first impression.
- Tone of voice impacts 38% of you overall first impression.
- Body language impacts 55% of your overall first impression.

The author of *Silent Messages,* Mehrabian abbreviates these influencers as the "3 Vs" for Verbal, Vocal, and Visual.

1. Verbal cues are those by which the listener will be measuring the quality of your presentation in terms of orga-

nization, content, and interest. Such cues account for only 7% of your first impression.

2. Vocal energy cues are those by which the interviewer will be measuring your level of enthusiasm, your clarity, your tone of voice, and your confidence. Such cues account for 38% of your first impression.

3. **Visual cues are the most important. They encompass body language, grooming, and business attire.** Such cues have the most impact in regard to your first impression. These factors account for 55% of your first impression. The good news is that of the three areas, you have personal control over improving and increasing your first impression here by upping your "likability" quotient.

Because they collectively make up 93% of the first impression you effect, I would like to take some time now to discuss the two highest-ranking areas: visual cues (55%) and vocal energy cues (38%).

### Visual (Body Language, Grooming, and Attire—55%)
Let's take the first area we can affect in a positive way and start to slant the cards your way: your visual appearance/cues.

Relative to these visual cues it's time to take a serious inventory and have a real heart to heart. Remember that you are the "product" and this is all just good, old-fashioned Marketing 101. Let's begin by talking about our packaging of the product: ourselves.

### Boost Your Visual Branding
If your clothes make you look different than your colleagues, then you have not been keeping up with the times. That means it's time for a transformation. Banish the thought, but your clothing could be making you appear older than you really are.

If you have not purchased a new one in the last 12 to 18 months, you should treat yourself to a new suit. Pick one that is stylish and current. When job interviewing, you want to look "with it," not outdated or old-fashioned. Since men's styles change less frequency, this is an area where it may be easier for the guys to fudge in than the ladies.

The most important point here is to make sure your clothes— all the way down to your shoes—do not make you look old. Ask your kids if they think you're dressing like an old fuddy-duddy. The reality will most likely lie somewhere in between their idea of current and yours. Study the late 20- to late 30-year-old professionals and see how they're dressing.

When picking your business clothes for an interview, stick with colors that are not just this season's "it" hues. Also avoid drab colors like brown. You want to look vibrant, though avoid really bright shades like neon green.

### For Executive Men Only

If you're a man, I would suggest going to a department store to purchase a new suit in an affordable price range. If you go to a nice outlet store, make sure you know a good tailor who will be able to ensure a perfect fit for a suit off the rack. The perfect tailored fit is what will make the look. Indeed, it will miraculously take five years off your appearance.

Trust me when I say there's nothing worse than a suit that is too tight or baggy. Try to stay with traditional grays or blues. Let the combination of the color of your eyes, hair, and skin tone guide you.

Also, make sure the shirt you select to go underneath does not fit too tightly around the neck. Your body may have changed since you last wore a dress shirt. It's important to own two that are current and fit!

As always, make sure your socks match the color of your trousers and are a plain dark color. (No argyles or gaudy prints!) Your shoes should always be freshly polished before every interview.

### For Executive Women Only

The point here is to not look old and frumpy. The same general rule applies to you as it does to the men. If you have not purchased a new suit in the last 12 months, then it's time to invest in one before hitting the interview circuit. Go to a department store for a good selection in an affordable price range. If you know a good seamstress or tailor, then by all means shop the high-end outlet stores.

The key is you want to look attractive, sophisticated, and stylish. With the exception of interviewing in a high-fashion industry, my suggestion is to avoid haute couture or trendy looks. They will be inappropriate for most industries and they will be outdated in a year.

Ladies fashions tend to change more often and to be more obvious in terms of age. I'm a firm believer that when it comes to investment pieces, you're better off steering toward classics. Pick pieces that will stand the test of time as opposed to being on the leading edge of fashion and being seen as too trendy. (There is one exception to this rule: In the housewares, consumer electronics, high-tech, gift, toy, cosmetics, and other similar industries you can pull off a higher-fashion look.)

Colors like navy or related shades will work well. Depending upon your overall skin coloring, look at red, black, tan, purple, brown, and yellow. Feel free to look at both my websites for business suggestions on women's apparel (www.ConsumerCareerSearch .com and www.TheJobSearchExperts.com).

I suggest you visit the foundation department in Nordstrom's. You will find wonderful experts there who will help take five years off your appearance, not to mention 5–10 pounds off your overall look, with the combination of a suit and various foundation products (e.g., bra, slip, body slimmer).

Choose shoes with a moderate but stylish heel. Again, I would suggest Nordstrom's or DSW as starting points.

Keep the jewelry simple, classy, and understated. Make sure your eyeglass frames are a current fashion style.

## Dated Hairstyles, Etc.

### *Men's Hair*

You should avoid a too short or buzz cut because it will look too harsh and age you. Always go to an interview well-groomed and freshly shaved. If you have a beard or mustache that has some gray in it, consider shaving it off. Another solution is to color it, but bear in mind this will require upkeep. This same recommendation applies to coloring the gray in your hair. Since men's hair is generally worn shorter than women's, you will need to be committed to keeping it touched up during the entire job search process.

1. Let me say that relative to interviewing, you're better off without a ponytail, beard, mustache, or long sideburns.

2. If you're really gray, consider getting some soft professional coloring to tone things down. Women have been doing this for years, but more and more men are showing up at the salons to have this process done. The trick is to not have the coloring/shading look too dark or fake. Another alternative is to buy a color rinse shampoo that will wash out eventually but cover the gray temporarily.

   If you're not comfortable with a dye job, then don't worry about it. Either way, I strongly suggest you go to a hair salon as opposed to a barbershop. It took me a while to talk my husband into the idea, but now he sees the difference in the cut of his hair.

### *Ladies' Hair*

For the ladies, I personally think gray hair can age you more than an outdated wardrobe. In addition to considering a touch-up, ask yourself how long you've had your current hairstyle.

I have some very dear friends who are still wearing their hair shoulder length and dyeing it the same color they had in their

20s. As you get older, you need to go with tones that are softer and warmer than your original color.

My hairdresser, Christy Dukewich, tells me that as we age, our skin tones and skin color lose some of their pigment tones. In other words, they become duller. You want a color that works with your changing skin tone and is warmer.

That natural change in your skin tone is another reason I suggest tasteful makeup for the ladies. If properly applied, understated makeup will make you look younger. In addition, most makeup today contains a UV protector, which is another way to slow down the aging process.

Relative to makeup, make sure you're wearing shades that are appropriate for your current skin tone and shape of your face. As we mature, it's not only our skin tone that changes. The shape of our face also alters. Again, I suggest you visit a department store or Sephora and take part in a free makeup session. You're bound to learn something new that will improve your appearance. Remember that the key here is to look vibrant, alive, energized, and young.

Be aware that certain makeup techniques can open up the appearance of your eyes, making your look wide awake and youthful. In addition, with the correct contouring techniques, you can very effectively improve the overall shape of your face.

Remember that as you age you will need to go softer on the color of your lips. As such, you should avoid harsh contrasting colors. The same is true for your blush color.

### Glasses

If you require reading glasses, make sure they're not the type of bifocals that have the line in the lens. This advice applies to both men and women. Purchase a new no-line pair that is current in design. This is yet another small way in which you can make yourself look younger.

For inspiration, study the styles the younger executives are wearing. Ask your optometrist for advice on a youthful-looking style. Otherwise, look at other people's glasses or pick up some magazines geared toward the 30-year-old.

### Teeth

Along this same line, consider whitening your teeth. You can have professional whitening done at your dentist's office or you can buy an at-home kit from the store. Do your research and consult with your dentist first. As they age, most people do see the color of the teeth aging right along with them.

### Weight

Let's address being older and overweight. It's a proven fact that as we age, our metabolism slows down. As a result, the tendency to pack on some unwanted extra pounds exists. The question is: How many unwanted pounds you have picked up and how well do you carry the excess weight?

Companies will never admit it, but there is a general bias against people who are overweight. The hiring authorities see obesity as a red flag for future health problems and thus organizational expenses. A general prejudice also exists that overweight people are lazy, not well-disciplined, and low in energy. For the most part, everything that is negative about excess weight represents a missed opportunity to make a positive first impression. If you're overweight, you need to overcome those concerns as much as possible.

Now is the time to get back to some basic exercise. Consult with your doctor first relative to taking on any new exercise program. Go to Halls Health Calculators and Charts or Blue Cross to figure out your ideal weight. Personally, I think ideal is relative to how you feel and a byproduct of your individual bone structure.

Set up some type of regular exercise routine, preferably three to four times per week. Regular dieting and exercise will go a long way toward giving you a trimmer appearance! Now is the time to work on that goal.

If that's not motivation enough, here's some more. Studies show that regular exercise will add three years to your life! It will also increase your energy level in addition to reducing the chance of a heart attack, stroke, and other debilitating conditions. Getting in shape with exercise is a definite win-win.

Everything we've discussed so far represents 55% of your first impression!

## Vocal (Enthusiasm, Clarity, Tone of Voice, and Confidence Level—38%)

When you first meet the person with whom you will be interviewing, always remember to give them a good solid handshake. Not one that is so strong as to cause the person discomfort or one that feels like a wet fish, mind you. Guys do not be afraid to give a solid handshake to a lady. Practice your handshake at home. Also, ladies, a nice solid handshake from you will speak volumes.

When you come into the interview room, if the interviewer offers you a choice of two chairs, pick the one that is firmer and which will be easier to get out of. If they offer you only one, take the one that you're offered.

When you sit down, don't collapse into the chair. Likewise, when it's time to leave, rise up from the chair with ease (even if you're having trouble).

Speak with a crisp, strong, well-modulated voice. Also remember to enunciate clearly and do not speak too quickly. It is human nature to speak too quickly when we're nervous.

Remember to look the person with whom you are interviewing directly in the eyes every time you answer them. Also remember to smile and open your eyes wide.

Take notes when appropriate, and use upbeat words in your answers. Respond with enthusiastic body movements as well.

When you master and improve both your visual and vocal first impressions, **you will have positively affected 93% of your first impression.** As a result, you will set a good strong tone for the potential working relationship.

## Biases

For whatever reason, some people may have a predetermined bias they carry against you in terms of being seriously considered as a viable candidate. What's worse, you probably won't even be aware of it. For example, your maturity, the color of your tie, even your first name could remind them of their ex-wife or something else distasteful you will never know about. Sometimes biases can be overcome while others you will never be able to sway.

For the sake of conversation, let's say that half of the people you will be interviewing with will be younger than you. If that is the case, then understand, realistically, they are most likely judging you. In all likelihood, they harbor some misconceptions about you as a viable candidate. You need to address as many of these misconceptions, prior to the interview, during the interview, and after the interview, as possible.

If you are aware that a possibility exists these biases dwell in the mind of your interviewer, then you can work on addressing them very subtlety.

### 10 Solutions to Overcome Negative Stereotype Concerns

Let's look at some specific concerns and how to address them.

1. "Older workers are unhealthy."

    *Solution:* You need to look fit and healthy. We have just discussed some of the aspects of your appearance you can address. In addition, take vitamins, and if you're a smoker, give up cigarettes.

2. "Older, overweight job seekers are lazy and lack motivation."

    *Solution:* Develop healthy eating and exercise habits, get in shape, and work on the product's packaging, you! They need to understand you are disciplined and motivated in all aspects of your life.

3. "Older workers don't have any energy."

*Solution:* The importance of regular exercise can't be stressed enough here. Not only will it make you look and feel better, but it will increase you energy level. In addition, take vitamins daily, maintain a healthy diet, and try energy drinks. All of these, particularly when combined with daily exercise, will give you the energy and drive employers are looking for.

To counter this perception, if possible during the interviewing process, describe all the activities you do in a normal business day. You might also mention how you worked late to solve a problem for your company.

4. "Older people know it all; they're set in their ways. They're not flexible."

   *Solution:* You need to be flexible to change, not tied to "how it used to be."

   To give yourself an edge, read the two to three latest books on new business management, productivity, and employee motivation. Stay current with the trends and changes taking place in your industry. Attend any industry trade shows or conventions when feasible. If possible, use some of the information you glean from these sources in some of your interview answers, assuming it's relevant to the topic.

   Be able to share a broad history perspective if appropriate. Also, discuss how you have worked on cross-generational teams.

5. "Older people's skills and education are not up-to-date."

   Non-Boomers automatically assume that Baby Boomers lack computer skills. They take for granted that a technology gap exists, even if it doesn't.

   *Solution:* Make sure you know how to use a computer, email, business software programs, Blackberry, iPhone, scan discs, etc. If you do not know how to use these products, then have your children, nephews, or nieces bring you up to speed fast!

If your technology skills are weak or outdated, now is the time to take a community college course or buy a book such as a "Dummies" guide.

If you're not as comfortable with your cell phone, texting, and other features, go to your cell phone vendor's store and have them teach you!

Last year, I had a 67-year-old executive whom I placed with a client. The client was concerned that the older gentleman might not know how to text. I explained that he had a Blackberry and knew how to fully use it. As a result, I was able to help my client overcome their pre-judgmental bias of the man's technical skills based on his age. In the end, the client hired him, and his technical skills have never been in issue at that job.

6. "Older people have slower brains."

*Solution:* Make sure you get a good night's sleep before the interview. I personally find sleep deprivation to have the single biggest impact on my memory.

Challenge yourself to learn a new software program, business skill, or language. It will show the interviewer you possess the ability to take on learning new skills and ideas with your brain.

Look into Ginkgo biloba, long-term use of vitamins A, E, and C, and evening primrose oil and seed. All are said to improve memory.

During the interview process, remember to focus on communicating to the hiring authority that you have a success record in accomplishing what they need done and that you get results! Use the SAR technique from the Powerful Resumes chapter (Situation, Action you took, and the Result that was achieved). You need to also remember to share your more recent professional results with the interviewer.

At all times, remember that people hire those they feel will make positive improvements to the organization. Those with a demonstrated and proven track record in following up and getting the needed results are particularly likely to score a job offer. You want the interviewer to understand that you can bring value to the organization by way of improvements and quality results. Those are the types of people organizations hire.

7. "Older people are using this job as a bridge to retirement."

   *Solution:* The average tenure with a company prior to this recent recession was four years. Unfortunately, it is now down to two years.

   Practice answers for questions like, "Where do you see yourself in five years?" Make sure you project a good, strong mental and physical energy level in your conversation by injecting lots of physical movement.

8. "Older workers will not be compatible with our younger clients and workers."

   *Solution:* Remember to mention how you have successfully participated on multigenerational teams. In addition, discuss your youth-oriented activities and stay current on world events, music, sports, and movies. Read the current business books and book reviews on management trends, team ideas, and industry trends. Stay current on industry buzzwords.

   If appropriate, you should be able to share that you are up-to-date on all the current business trends and current events.

   In your pre-contact/pre-interview company research, you should have been able to define somewhat the type of culture that exists there. That being the case, if you're talking to them, we can assume that based on what you know about their culture and environment, this is a place where you would like to work.

Share you work-related results and communicate to the interviewer professional examples where you success-fully worked with younger bosses and team members.

*And finally the two biggies . . .*

9. "Older workers are overqualified in terms of experience."
   *Solution*: Ask them point blank what they mean by "overqualified." This straightforwardness will give you a chance to address their concerns directly, right on the spot. Remember, however, not to come off defensive or confrontational.

   One possible answer is, "I like to see myself as the best qualified instead of overqualified." Another is, "I don't see myself as overqualified. I just believe that you'll be getting more bang for the buck."

   However you choose to respond, answer with a positive statement about your qualifications.

### RESUME ADVICE FOR THE 45+ CROWD

Relative to your resumes, here are some ways to soften the issue of age to get yourself in the door. The goal is to have the hiring authority focus on your accomplishments and what you bring to the party. You want to detract them from getting hung up on your age.

In addition, make sure you're applying for positions that you're actually qualified for. If you are willing to take a step down the corporate ladder, you may need to tone down your resume somewhat. Also, have a good solid answer ready on the sound logic behind this step-down that you can supply during the interview.

Descending the corporate ladder may make sense for a number of reasons (e.g., changing industries and geographic reasons like wanting to move to a specific location or being unwilling to relocate and wanting to stay where you are for personal reasons). The important thing here is your ability to communicate a solid, logical reason for your decision.

For more tips on how to overcome age bias on your resume, refer to the Secrets to a Powerful Resume chapter.

10. "Older workers are overpriced in terms of salary."

*Solution:* Counter this perception with, "I value challenge and relationships. Salary is not my sole consideration. I'm definitely interested in this position." Or try this line of reasoning: "I feel that if we want to work together, money will not be an issue. You strike me as a fair person."

Make sure you check out websites such as the following to confirm what your realistic compensation is.

- www.Salary.com
- www.Jobnob.com
- www.JobSearchIntelligence.com
- www.Payscale.com
- www.SalaryExpert.com
- www.SalaryList.com

If you are overpriced, try such strategies as negotiating a sign-on bonus or a six-month salary review, etc. Refer to the How to Negotiate the Salary You Want and Deserve in This Current Market chapter for additional advice.

In addition, point out that:
- Salary is only part of your employment motivations.
- You are flexible regarding salary
- You've done your research with respect to the position's salary range potential.

### 6 Advantages the "Mature" Job Seeker Offers the Perspective Employer
#### (Your True Value and Benefit to the Employer)

By now you're probably thinking that if you're 45+ years of age, you're fighting an uphill battle. But there are many job-related plusses that come with age!

1. Wisdom—Age brings wisdom with it. Because of your maturity, you are able to recognize both success and failure. Your experience can provide insight into the future.

2. Superior work ethic—It's a commonly accepted fact that Baby Boomers possess a proven track record of good solid work ethics in addition to being dependable. They are also known for being loyal to their employers, often more so than their younger co-workers.

3. You have a mature attitude and life experience in handling various types of crisis on the job—Because of your proven experience; you have developed a good solid head when it comes to crisis and problem-solving.

4. Strong mentoring capabilities—You're a natural role model to those who are younger than you.

5. Less likelihood for maternity leave or significant time off for sick kids or their after-school activities.

6. An understanding of the importance of good follow-up, customer service, and developing a genuine rapport with people as opposed to establishing relationships via email

Remember that a lot of age is a mindset. "The majority of it is between the ears."

You will not be able to change everyone's mindset on the "older worker," but you may be able to alter the perception of quite a few people with some of the ideas shared in this chapter.

Remember that you can impact 93% of your first impression during the interview. What's more, you can do so by simply improving your vocal and visual presentation. Thankfully, you have control over both these areas. To use this information presented in this chapter to your best advantage, you must get organized and apply its advice. Most job seekers do not know this, so leveraging this information gives you an automatic competitive advantage

Good luck in using what I have shared in this chapter to make your job search a successful one!

In the reader Bonus Material for this chapter, you will find a list of resource books to gain additional information on this subject. In particular, they'll teach you how to improve your "visual imaging" for the interviewing process.

*Age should not have its face lifted, but it should*
*rather teach the world to admire wrinkles as the etchings*
*of experience and the firm lines of character.*
—Ralph Barton Perry

*The secret to staying young is to live honestly,*
*eat slowly, and just not think about your age.*
—Lucille Ball

*In youth we learn; in age we understand.*
—Marie von Ebner-Eschenbach

*Live your life and forget your age.*
—Frank Bering

## Job Search Action Plan

1 Take the reader Bonus Material for this chapter, "Job Search Experts 45+ Suggested Book List," to your library. Check out 2–3 books that appear to have helpful information. Read these books and see where you can improve your "visual packaging."

2 Read "Never Too Young or Too Old" in your reader Bonus Material for this chapter.

3 Talk to your doctor about getting back in shape if you are not currently at your fittest.

4 Work a plan that will improve your visual packaging and your energy level.

# Job Search
# Success Strategy

# Game Plan: How to Succeed with Your Job Search in This New Economy

*The person who succeeds is not the one*
*who holds back, fearing failure, nor the*
*one who never fails . . . but rather the*
*one who moves on in spite of failure.*

—CHARLES SWINDOLL

I KNOW THIS CURRENT LABOR MARKET is the most challenging one you have ever been involved in while looking for a job. Because of this tendency, it will take more motivation and strength of heart to succeed than it would in a more robust economy.

The key to your success is to know your goal, keep a positive mindset, and never ease up on your intense commitment to landing that next great job!

Follow my Job Search Success System™ as outlined in the book and you'll achieve that success!

1. Have a good, solid core belief in yourself and your end goal.

2. Create strong customized, accomplishment-oriented resumes and letters for each specific job and interview you are responding to.

3. Create and constantly update your target company list.

4. Cultivate a strong networking base that you stay in touch with and also keep updated on your job search. Remember once you land a job to also stay in contact with your network on a fairly regular basis. Also remember to be genuine and real at all times.

5. Work on constantly updating and adding to your hidden market company list. This is the list you will use with your informational interviews and broadcast letters.

6. Continue to improve your target company, networking, and hidden market company lists on a consistent basis. It is from these lists that you build your pipelines for your job search leads.

7. Prepare in advance for every interview in terms of customized resumes, letters, company research, and interview questions.

8. Confirm that you are well-versed and comfortable with the strength of your answers for the hypothetical interview questions you have practiced prior to each new interview.

9. Remember to be ***meticulous*** with all your follow-up and follow-through following all conversations and meetings regarding your job search.

10. Do not stop or slow down on any of these steps in your Job Search Success System. Keep your pipeline full and keep working that pipeline.

Remember your job search is not over until you have a physical offer in hand and have accepted and started your new job.

Most job seekers slack off when:

1. They get discouraged, rejected, and turned down.

2. They think they are close to an offer.

You never want to slow down the process of filling your pipeline until 30 days after you are on the job and you know everything is working out.

The system I have shared with you in this book is a tried and true system that has worked for many, many people, just like you, whom I have helped over the years.

The Job Search Success System™ I have shared with you in this book is a new system I have specifically customized to increase results for you in this new economy.

In this book, if you follow this system, you will have learned how to differentiate yourself from the crowd and how to find the job leads where there is no "crowd."

Trust yourself and trust the system. I know it will work for you. It has worked for everyone I have shared it with who has been truly committed to success in their job search.

I know you too will succeed if you are truly committed. I believe in you!

I wish you the best of everything, achievement of all the success you want, and happiness for you and your family.

Blessings,

Eleanor

The Executive Job Search Expert™

# Job Search Success Bonus Materials and Additional Bonus Resources

## Extra Special Bonus Materials Only for Book Readers

THIS MATERIAL IS KEY TO YOU, the reader, succeeding faster in your job search than those who are not reading this book. Following is a series of Bonus Materials specially designed to assist those of you who are truly committed to succeeding in your job search! I am now sharing some of my "tricks of the trade" with you.

Register NOW to receive your free Job Search Experts Gift Resources: www.thejobsearchexperts.com/book-readers-bonus-materials/.

Congratulations on taking the next step forward in transforming your job search and taking the game up a notch!

I look forward to working with you and personally helping you with your job search.

It is an honor to serve you and be part of your job search success.

Warmly,

*Eleanor*

Eleanor Anne Sweet
The Executive Job Search Expert™

**Additional Job Search Expert Resources**
Visit my website for additional information:
www.TheJobSearchExperts.com

This website is designed for you, the job seeker who is actively looking for new employment or soon to be looking for a new position. This site offers expert job search informational-based resources, products, and coaching programs to assist you with your job search.

Go to www.TheJobSearchExperts.com to register for our free gift. You can also sign up for future email invitations to our special job search expert events and to receive helpful tips.

 *Specifically for Consumer Products Executives:*
www.TheRemingtonGroup.com
The Remington Group is an executive-retained search firm specializing in placing consumer products executives both nationally and internationally. Your resume is never presented to any of our clients unless we contact you first and receive your permission directly.

Send your confidential resumes to: sweet@TheRemington Group.com.

 www.ConsumerCareerSearch.com
The Consumer Career Search is a web-posting site designed specifically for consumer products manufacturers to post positions directly. It provides consumer product executives with the ability to apply directly to these openings once they are registered in our private database, which is not publically mined.

To create your confidential "Private Profile" for future postings, go to "sign up": www.consumercareersearch.com/Candidates.aspx.

Alternatively, go directly to: www.consumercareersearch.com/Candidate_SignUp.aspx.

www.GreatInterviewQuestionsBlog.com
The Great Interview Blog does just what it says. It offers great interview questions and suggested answers to assist you in maximizing your interview process with the hiring executive. Here you will find great tips, advice, and strategies to help you become stronger as an effective interviewer. As a result, you will rise to the next level in the job search process!

Go to www.GreatInterviewQuestionsBlog.com to register for you free gift. You can also sign up for future email mailings containing great interview question tips.

Also plan to visit my latest web site:

 www.AskTheJobSearchExpert.com
Submit to me directly your single most pressing question you have regarding how to succeed in your job search, and I will email you back your answer. You will automatically be registered for my mailing list for future monthly open live Q&A sessions.

Feel free to connect with me on LinkedIn at:

 www.linkedin.com/pub/eleanor-anne-sweet/0/614/253.

Visit the following link for the contact information of my mentors, coaches, and professional support team who helped me on my journey of creating this book to help better serve you, my reader, the job seeker:

 www.thejobsearchexperts.com/my-professional-resources/.

# Special Advice for Success Oriented Executives

## Executive Job Search Success

JOB SEARCH EXPERT ADVICE for the truly motivated, success oriented and ambitious executive . . .

Take your job search to the next level . . .

Time to notch up the game!

Learn more about our popular Job Search Success System Coaching, where I personally take you under my wing and work with you one-on-one to implement all the tools included in this course.

In this powerful online course, complete with live training sessions, you'll discover easy-to-implement strategies that will help you get where you need to go to land that next great job!

Research has shown that when a job seeker is part of a coaching program, they achieve faster results in landing that next great job. Be part of a team!

Go to:

www.TheJobSearchExperts.com

I personally look forward to "meeting" you as a member of one of our coaching programs on my live calls and helping you transform your job search results!

Start your engine,

Eleanor Anne Sweet

The Executive Job Search Expert™

P.S.

You can reach me at sweet@TheJobSearchExperts.com or 847-304-4500 for details on our other coaching programs, to discover which one will serve your current needs best.

# ABOUT THE AUTHOR

ELEANOR ANNE SWEET, "The Executive Job Search Expert," is a 23-year veteran of over 587 executive search projects with a 99.8% success rate. She has studied success and leadership and its effect on organizations ranging from privately held firms to major Fortune 500 corporations. She has spent the majority of her professional career helping the best and brightest consumer products executive professionals in America find great companies to work for both domestically and internationally.

Eleanor has been quoted in the *Wall Street Journal* in addition to major trade journals and other leading publications. She has authored *Instant Job Leads #1* and *Job Search New Career Ideas*.

Eleanor Anne Sweet has an MBA (EMP) from Kellogg Graduate School of Management at Northwestern University. She received her undergraduate degree from Boston College with a B.S. in Marketing.

Eleanor started her professional career with GE Lighting and Salton in a marketing and sales management capacity.

She is also the President and owner of The Remington Group, a retained executive search firm that has specialized in placing consumer products executives nationally and internationally since 1987.

In addition, she is the founder of www.ConsumerCareerSearch. com, the first job posting website exclusively designed for the consumer products industry. Consumer Career Search was launched in March 2006.

www.ConsumerCareerSearch.com was designed as an easy-to-use, internet-based human resource tool for those consumer products companies that would prefer to post their career positions before committing to a traditional customized search.

In February 2010, she launched the website www.The JobSearchExperts.com, which is specifically designed for the executive job seeker who is looking for professional tools and support to assist and accelerate their job search process.

On a personal note, Eleanor was unemployed twice and understands the challenges of a job search firsthand! In addition, her husband became unemployed in this new economy.

Eleanor was born and raised in the greater Cleveland, Ohio area. She is 100% "Made in America." She resides in the Northwest suburbs of Chicago with her husband, daughter, son, and three cats.

To find out more about Eleanor's workshops, training, coaching, books, and audio training programs, or to inquire about her availability as a speaker or trainer, you can contact her office at:

The Job Search Experts.com
200 Applebee Street, Suite 213
Barrington, Il 60010
Phone: 847-304-4500 fax: 847-304-4505
sweet@TheJobSearchExperts.com
www.TheJobSearchExperts.com
The Experts in Job Search Solutions.™

*Sweet Success Publishing*
*Fawn Elias*
*Chief Corporate Mascot*
*1996–2011*

# PS—It is all about helping . . .

I personally have always felt that we are all in this world to help each other in one way or another. I hope that my book has helped transform your job search and you are on the way to landing that next great job you are looking for.

In the spirit of supporting those in need, I have selected the American Cancer Society to receive a portion of the profits that are generated from the sale of this book, *The NEW Rules of Job Search—How to Land an Executive Job in the New Economy*.

Many of us have lost a loved one to cancer. I lost my own father, Ray Elias in six months to Acute Myeloid Leukemia (AML).

I have been personally involved helping my local American Cancer Society group and Relay for Life. It is a great and rewarding experience.

Join the fight against cancer by donating today to the American Cancer Society.

It is all about "Celebrating More Birthdays."

**American Cancer Society—The Official Sponsor of Birthdays®**
If you would like to help support the American Cancer Society, you can send a tax deductible contribution to:

American Cancer Society
P.O.Box 22538
Oklahoma City, OK 73123-1538

Make checks payable to "American Cancer Society."
If you prefer you can make your donation directly
over the phone at 1-800-227-2345.

I appreciate you joining me in making a difference with finding a cure for cancer.

Thank you for helping more people "Celebrate Birthdays."

Warmly,
Eleanor Anne Sweet

**WITHDRAWN**

Made in the USA
San Bernardino, CA
09 March 2014